PART ONE

THE
ISLE OF MAN
RAILWAY

St John's. Wednesday, 20th September 1962. Blowing off energetically, Isle of Man Railway 2-4-0T No.**10** *G.H.Wood*, re-railing jack prominent on the right-hand side tank, draws into the Down side of the gravelled island platform of this attractive junction station which, like its counterparts world-wide, alternated between periods of intense activity and sleepy calm. On a balmy day of 'Indian Summer' the porter, with that inate courtesy so much a part of the Manx character, assists a family party, complete with perambulator to entrain for their afternoon jaunt to Peel. *Norman Jones.*

COMPILED and WRITTEN by

NORMAN JONES

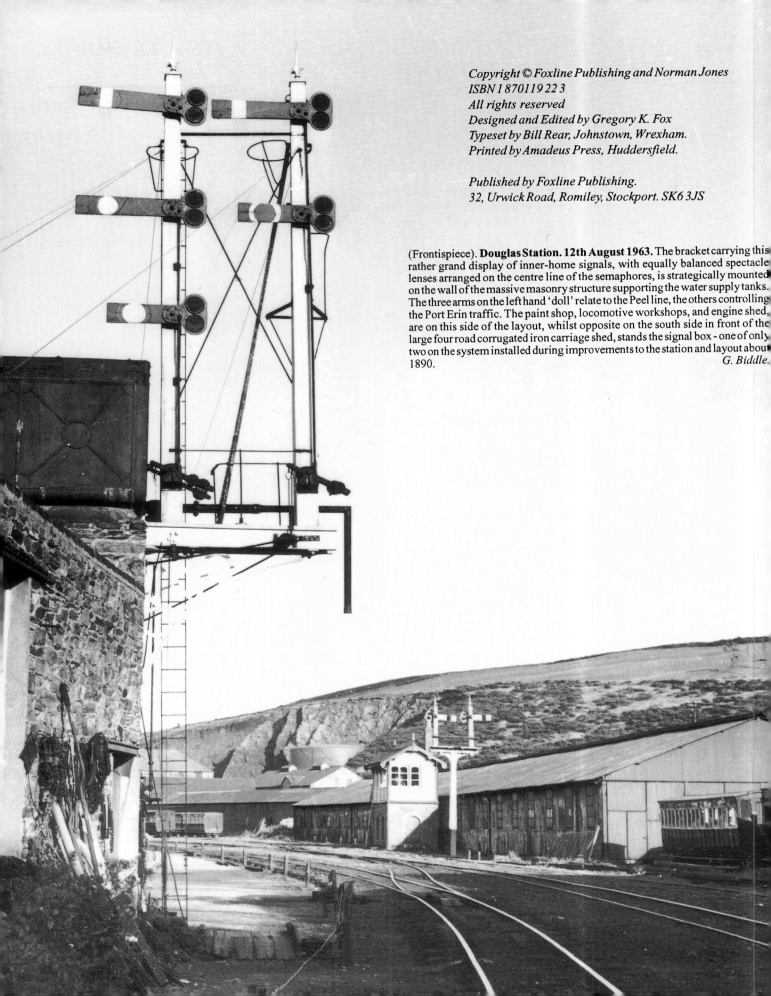

Designed and Edited by Gregory K. Fox
Typeset by Bill Rear, Johnstown, Wrexham.
Printed by Amadeus Press, Huddersfield.

Published by Foxline Publishing.
32, Urwick Road, Romiley, Stockport. SK6 3JS

(Frontispiece). **Douglas Station. 12th August 1963.** The bracket carrying this rather grand display of inner-home signals, with equally balanced spectacle lenses arranged on the centre line of the semaphores, is strategically mounted on the wall of the massive masonry structure supporting the water supply tanks. The three arms on the left hand 'doll' relate to the Peel line, the others controlling the Port Erin traffic. The paint shop, locomotive workshops, and engine shed, are on this side of the layout, whilst opposite on the south side in front of the large four road corrugated iron carriage shed, stands the signal box - one of only two on the system installed during improvements to the station and layout about 1890.
G. Biddle.

16th July 1962. When No.8 *Fenella* took her turn before the lens, dainty, with her unmistakeable copper-capped "Beyer, Peacock" chimney with its brass numeral, that she was of an earlier period was undoubted and the works plate, parallel with but in rear of the nameplate (burnished brass letters on a red background) proclaimed that she was Gorton built in 1894 - Works No.3610. Like sister engine No.6 *Peveril*, she took her name from a character in Sir Walter Scott's book, so popular with Victorian readers, "Peveril of the Peak". Differences between the front-end of No.8 and No.10 are apparent, especially the presence of a Displacement Feed Lubricator that required regular attention and frequent topping up. Railway modellers especially may be interested in details of the leading Bissel, or "pony" truck, also the guard irons, driving wheel brake shoes and linkages etc. *Fenella* arrived with the bell-mouthed dome and Salter valves of her clan, and retained these until 1937 when "modernised", by the acquisition of a closed dome and "pop" valves. However, she still retains her look of Victorian elegance and charm.   *Norman Jones.*

The Manxman

Refreshment Car Express

LONDON (Euston) and LIVERPOOL (Lime Street)

WEEKDAYS				Mons. to Fris.	Sats.
London (Euston) .. .. ..dep	am 10 30	Liverpool (Lime Street) dep.		pm 2†10	pm 2† 0
		Rugby (Midland) ..arr		4§14	4 11
Liverpool (Lime Street) .. ..arr	pm 2* 5	London (Euston) .. ,,		5§45	5 45

*—On Saturdays arrives 2.15 pm.   A connecting steamer for Douglas, Isle of Man, leaves Liverpool (Landing Stage) each weekday at 3.30 pm until 13th September (inclusive) and also on 18th September.

†—Passengers from Isle of Man by Isle of Man Steam Packet Co.'s steamer leave Douglas 9.0 am.

§—On Fridays arrives Rugby (Midland) 4.19 pm and London (Euston) 5.50 pm.

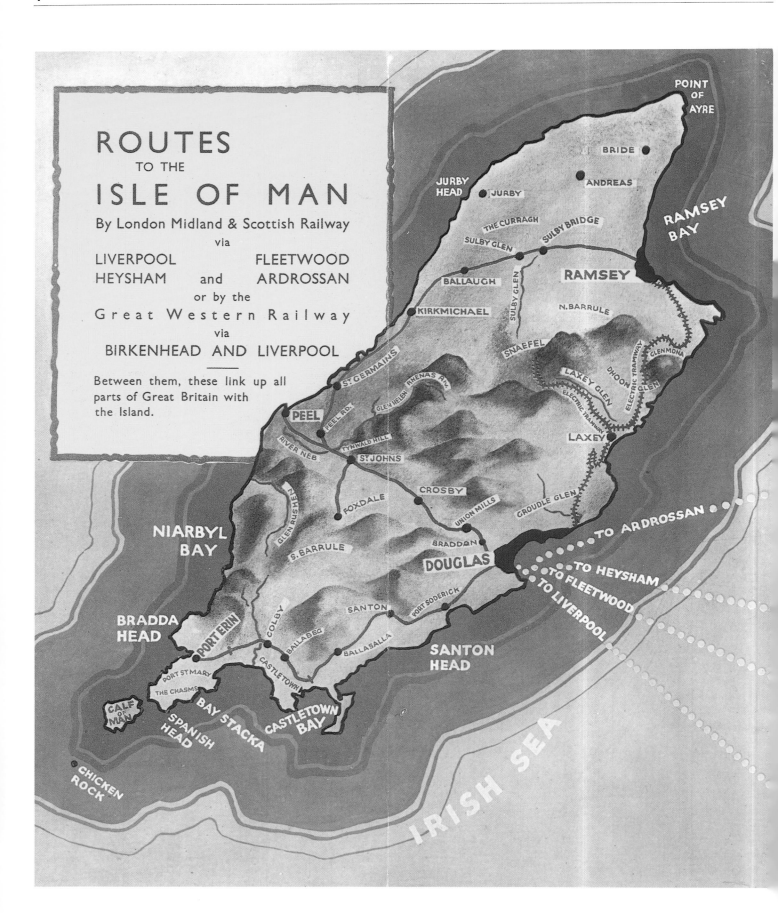

ROUTES
TO THE
ISLE OF MAN

By London Midland & Scottish Railway

via

LIVERPOOL   **FLEETWOOD**
HEYSHAM   and   **ARDROSSAN**

or by the

Great Western Railway

via

BIRKENHEAD AND LIVERPOOL

Between them, these link up all parts of Great Britain with the Island.

t John's. Monday 16th July 1962. Beyer Peacock built 2-4-0T No.10 *G.H.Wood,* Works No.4662 of 1905 enters the station with a Peel - Douglas bound train.
our wheeled carriages were ordered for the opening of the line to Peel in 1873, but only three years later six new bogie carriages had arrived from Brown Marshalls
Co.,Ltd. F5 featured here, is an example of the small class F1-F6; as new the interior layout was G/3/1/1/33, but by 1962 it had been changed to G/3/1/1/3/3.
he diamond frame bogies, 25 ft 10 ins apart each had a wheelbase of 4 ft 6 ins and the bodies were 35 ft long, by 7 ft wide and measured 9 ft 4 ins from rail level
o roof. *Norman Jones.*

The Beginning. The 2-4-0 Tanks.

An almost mythical batch of locomotives with steeply inclined outside
ylinders was that built for the Metropolitan Railway by Messrs Beyer,
eacock and Co., of Gorton in the 1880's, but their close relatives were eight
-4-0 tank engines and forty one 2-4-0 tender engines which in 1862 Gorton
upplied to the Spanish Tudela and Bilbao Railway.

hat some 'Crewe' features were present stemmed from the participation
n their design of Thomas Hunt Esq., a former Manager at Crewe Works, who
eft England to become Locomotive Superintendent of the Spanish Rail-
vay. The first batch of Bilbao 2-4-0's had fixed leading wheels but a
ubsequent order called for the substitution of a 'Bissel' bogie or 'pony' truck
ased on a design patented in 1857.

he 'Tudela' type of engine with its sloping cylinders proved to be an
xcellent machine, so much so that derivatives of the basic pattern were
uilt for various gauges. At this time both standard and 3ft 6ins gauge lines
vere under construction by the Norwegian government; 24 miles of the
atter (n.g.) ran from Grundsett to Hamar, and two years later a further 30

miles was laid between Trondheim and Storen. Engines from Messrs.
Robert Stephenson & Co., of Newcastle-on-Tyne and Messrs. Slaughter
Grunning of Bristol worked on the Grundsett and Trondheim lines respectively, then, in 1865, Messrs Beyer, Peacock & Co., entered into complicated
and lengthy but, eventually eminently successful negotiations with the
Engineer of the Norwegian Government Railways, Carl Pihl Esq., for the
supply of a version of the now popular 2-4-0T engines. Twenty-seven of the
class were built initially, for Norway. A rather exotic version adorned with
cow-catcher and spark-arrester chimney went to South America, but
probably the most definitive and (certainly nowadays) best known exam-
ples were the 4-4-0 standard gauge tanks for the Metropolitan Railway and
the energetic little 3ft 0ins gauge 2-4-0 tanks of the Isle of Man Railway Co.,
still delighting visitors to their island home, and running nowadays under
the banner of the Transport Division of the Isle of Man Department of
Tourism and Transport, who are also responsible for the Manx Electric
Railway, the Snaefell Mountain Railway and also operate regular bus
services throughout the year to towns all over the island.

The Mersey Scene. 16th July 1962. Viewed from the navigating bridge of the Isle of Man Steam Packet Co.'s 'Classic' steamer Snaefell (Captain J.D.Craine about to leave Prince's Stage on the long standing morning sailing to Douglas. For more than a century, then, Liverpool had contended with London for the title of Great Britain's premier port. Unlike the present day scene, the river was alive with esturial tugs working their tows between the kaleidoscope of docks and warehouses, and handsome cargo liners, long gone to foreign breakers, lay off in the river, awaiting admission to their pre-determined berth. The Port of Liverpool has adapted to modern trends and huge container ships, their unsightly deck cargoes stacked high, have replaced the supremely handsome but labour intensive break-bulk cargo liners. Along with those ships, have vanished many of the illustrious shipping firms long household names to Liverpudlians. Gone also this last two decades, are the three miles of docks which, from Liverpool's Pier Head, Salthouse and Canning Docks stretched southwards to end at Harrington and Herculaneum. Nevertheless, from 1st October 1984 Liverpool has had the status of being a Freeport and has a new dock, the Royal Seaforth, designed to handle the very latest designs of ships. The entrance is 130 feet in width. The dock, triangular in shape, having 85 acres of water area and overall quay length of 1,200 yards. Vessels enter the new complex via the river lock and the Gladstone area of docks and, following a period of absence when the service was transferred to Heysham, there is again an I.O.M.S.P. presence at Liverpool, sailing from the smaller, new stage, which has replaced the much lamented but ageing and life-expired Prince's Floating Stage. *Norman Jones*

Liverpool. 16th July 1962. T.S.S. *Snaefell* lying alongside the Prince's Landing Stage. To make good the losses sustained during World War II and to replace the ageing vessels which had maintained the island's essential services throughout that period, contracts were placed with Messrs Cammell Laird's of Birkenhead by the I.O.M.S.P.Co.for a class of fast and modern turbine steamers with fine lines enhanced by raked stems, cruiser sterns, single cowl-topped funnels and two masts. The first two 'sisters' *King Orry IV* and *Mona's Queen IV* came out in 1946, *Tynwald V* appearing in 1947 and *Snaefell V* in 1948. The latter was withdrawn in 1977 and broken up at Blyth in 1978. Passengers view the shipping off Birkenhead docks as on *Snaefell's* foredeck the lines are being 'singled' ready for departure. The massive ventilator is a notable feature, as is the tripod mast supporting the brightly burnished ship's bell, with pendant from the tongue, a fine example of pipeclayed ornamental ropework. Man made fibres are absent from the fine assembly of hempen ropes, note too the closed mesh screens fitted as added protection to the deck rails. Standing vertically beneath the ratlines is one of the traditional rattan fenders lowered over the side as a vessel approached her berth, it was considered most unseaman-like for them to dangle outboard when a ship was under way. *Norman Jones.*

Getting There, The Crossing.

With names such as *Ben-my-Chree, Mona's Isle, King Orry* and *Tynwald* there has always been a fine euphony and panache in the names borne by vessels of the Isle of Man Steam Packet Company Ltd, a shipping line that celebrated its 150th birthday in 1980 and within the span of its first one hundred years of existence played a significant role in raising the condition of it's homeland from a condition of penury to that of an immensely popular and respected tourist resort.

The Vikings were amongst the first tourists to visit Mona's Isle, and the early paddle steamers of the company, with their sea-kindly hulls and graceful lines, bespoke an affinity with the Norse long-boats. Peel sadly no longer has any rail connection with Douglas, but the former Isle of Man Railway goods shed is now the 'Odin Raven' boathouse and houses a replica of a Viking longboat, which was built in Norway and sailed to the Isle of Man as part of the Tynwald Millennium celebrations in 1979. A colourful character George "King of the Vikings", wearing the dress of a warrior, complete with a helmet crowned with a pair of ferocious horns (shades of Eddie Grundy of The Archers and Ambridge), is usually around in season to greet visitors.

The eleventh century brought to Mann, Godred Crovan the fabled King Orry, credited with being the founder of Tynwald, the open-air parliament. Manx history has been turbulent, amongst its notable invaders being Robert the Bruce who came before Bannockburn. The island knew, also, the strife of the Cromwellian period and it is no wonder that, having afforded enforced hospitality to so many unwelcome guests that by 1736, when the sovereignty had passed to the second Duke of Atholl, the inhabitants were mainly dependant upon marginal farming, fishing and the contraband trade for their livelihood.

Communications with the mainland consisted of occasional visits by ships from Liverpool and Whitehaven, and monthly calls from two, 60 ton trading loops, but in 1765 the sovereignty passed to the English Crown and two years later the British Government put a weekly mail packet boat on the Whitehaven-Douglas station. Trade expanded and besides the occasional traders, six 400 ton burthen vessels called fortnightly but the passage from Whitehaven, which in good weather took about six hours, was often hazardous. In 1813 the sailing packet *Duchess of Atholl,* Liverpool bound

with passengers and cargo, spent three days and nights at sea; she got within sight of the approaches to Liverpool but was driven back to the Isle of Man and landed her passengers at Derbyhaven. On 16th January 1819, the sailing packet *Lord Hill* was less fortunate, foundering near the mouth of the Ribble with the loss of passengers and crew.

But the day of the steamship was dawning, bringing a progressive reduction in the hazards of the crossing; even before the *Lord Hill* calamity the Liverpool Mercury reported the arrival on June 28th 1815 of the steamer *Elizabeth.* That legendary steamer the *Comet* of 1812 was built in Glasgow by John Wood with machinery by John Robertson and was 40ft in length with a beam of 10ft 6ins. The *Elizabeth*, also Clyde built but by Thomson, was rather larger with a length of 50ft, beam of 11ft and cabin accommodation. She plied daily between Glasgow and Greenock until her sale to Liverpool interests, and in the early morning of her arrival at Liverpool had called in at Ramsey, so making her, it is believed, the first steamer in Manx waters. This same wooden paddle steamer was destined for the Liverpool-Runcorn station (and possibly Warrington although her presence so far up stream has not been established.) The quays at Runcorn were the transhipment point for passengers and freight from Manchester, and points inland, travelling thence on 'Mersey flats' via the Mersey & Irwell Navigation and Runcorn & Latchford Canal, or along the Duke of Bridgewater's fine broad canal. Unfortunately the *Elizabeth* was not a financial success for her proprietors, a syndicate managed by Lieutenant Colin Watson of the East Yorkshire Militia, for they soon disposed of her to new owners who in an endeavour to reduce the running costs carried out an amazing modification to her machinery. The boiler and steam engine were removed and she was fitted with a horizontal circular 'gin' which was rotated by horses, a simple mechanism transferring the drive to the paddle wheels. However the *Elizabeth* was no more successful in this guise, the horses (as might have been expected) either becoming seasick or unable to maintain their feet when the vessel rolled. In the same period (1816) the steamer *Greenock* bound from the Clyde to the Mersey is reported to have dallied in Manx waters undertaking a pleasure trip from Laxey. However, despite the incursions of steamships into other coastal waters, sailing packets continued to carry Manx mails until 1825.

St John's. 20th September 1962. No.**10**.*G.H.Wood.* at the head of a train on the Peel line eases gently over the level crossing of the Kirkmichael - Castletown road where it will halt with the rear end clear of a trailing connection for a wagon to be attached. The land to the right of the other (Ramsey) line was once the site of the original Manx Northern's St John's station.F5 the leading coach had spoked wheels and a single, transverse bogie spring.
Norman Jones.

St John's. 20th September 1962. The fireman looks back from the cramped footplate as under the gaze of his wife and an interested onlooker, Stationmaster the late George Crellin watches the M Class wagon being attached to the rear of the Peel bound train. Closer inspection proves the wagon to be rather dilapidated, a side-plank is missing from the drop side and the bolts in the bow-end supports are rusty and corroded. A prominent foreground feature is the Stevens Patent Signal Lever a typical, yet effective and reliable example of convoluted Victorian mechanical ingenuity.
Norman Jones.

Peel Harbour and Station. 20th September 1962. The ex County Donegal railcars, following the northwards curving course of the River Neb to enter the environs of Peel, have passed the site of the old ropeworks building, the power station and brick works, to negotiate the aromatically smoky odour of the kipper factory, and enter station limits via the gated level crossing over Mill Road, as Working No. 14, the 2.10 pm Douglas - Peel (arr. 2.45 pm). A feature of the livery is that the white waist band continued in a straight line across the facing 'Douglas' end dips in a pronounced chevron at what will be the 'trailing' end. *Norman Jones.*

Peel. 20th September 1962. The lines operated by the County Donegal Railways Joint Committee closed to all traffic on 1st January 1960; diesel railcars No.s. **19** and **20** were just over 10 years old when they were purchased by the I.O.M.Rly and landed at Douglas on 7th May 1961. Wagon M56 is now securely attached and will be drawn out and then propelled into the passenger platform to load parcels traffic, and we note the waist line dipping in a chevron at this end of the pair. And the posters: Excursions to Dublin and Belfast for only £1.2.6 (£1.25), Ivy Benson and her Ladies Band at the Villa Marina and Wrestling at Derby Castle were only some of the delights on offer. **Those were the days!** *Norman Jones*

[above]

Liverpool. 16th July 1962. T.S.S. *Snaefell V* the purser on the stage and 2nd Officer at the head of the gangway, welcome Douglas bound passengers aboard. Like the other post-war 'classic steamers' Snaefell V was 344 ft 3 ins. L.O.A. and 325 ft 0 ins. B.P. with an extreme breadth of 47 ft 8 ins., depth 17 ft 2 ins. and 12 ft 6 ins. S.L.L., but differing from the King Orry V and Mona's Queen IV in having windows on the shelter deck carried aft. The Manx emblem adorns her bows and also the red house-flag, on which it was displayed centrally, flanked by the letters I O M S P C, in yellow. She was capable of steaming at 21 knots (24.18 m.p.h.) and with a crew of 68 was certified for 2,163 passengers. When cars were carried as deck cargo passenger numbers were reduced on a pro-rata basis. Snaefell V and Mona's Isle V were the last Steam Packet ships to work the Heysham to Douglas service before it was withdrawn, moreover Snaefell V became a great favourite on the Douglas to Llandudno and other routes taken over by the I.O.M.S.P. from the Liverpool & North Wales Steamship Company Ltd., which went into voluntary liquidation in 1962.   *Norman Jones.*

[left]

T.S.S. *Snaefell* (Navigating Bridge). 16th July 1962. With the buildings of New Brighton, which still had its pier and floating landing stage extant in view on the port side. However, to the right of the photograph, the late Captain J.D. Craine has rung down 'Full Speed Ahead' on the engine room telegraph. Interesting features are the massive well-scrubbed gratings underfoot, the hefty proportions of the foremast and the jumper wire running through stanchions, on which a canvas dodger could be rigged in foul weather conditions. Captain Craine wore leather gloves as did most masters, a precaution against tarnishing the well burnished brasswork of the telegraph instruments. The protective canvas cover shields the manoeuvring, or berthing telegraph. The author recalls polishing ships brasswork with a fearsome mixture of powdered bath-brick and colza oil which was very effective in removing skin from the hands as well as verdigris from copper surfaces.   *Norman Jones.*

The Steam Era

For years James Little of Greenock was engaged with sea-borne traffic between the mainland and Isle of Man, the population of which increased in proportion to its prosperity, from 20,000 in 1767 to 40,000 in 1829.

In 1822 vessels of the powerful St. George Steam Packet Co., began sailing between Liverpool and Douglas and although the summer services were adequate, Manxmen thought the winter sailings unsatisfactory. Furthermore, the steamers offered only the most rudimentary shelter for passengers so in 1826 an attempt was made to float a shipping company with Manx capital.

This attempt failed and it seemed that the St. George Company would remain in command of the station but on 17th December 1829, a meeting was held in Douglas hopefully to raise sufficient capital to start a Manx owned Douglas to Liverpool passenger and mail steamer service.

This attempt was successful and the Mona's Isle Company was formed. The company's first vessel the P.S. *Mona's Isle* was of wooden construction Clyde built by John Wood and Company and launched on 30th June 1830. Amidst scenes of great excitement and rejoicing she arrived in Douglas about six weeks later. Of 200 tons gross her dimensions were, length 116ft., beam 19ft, draught 10ft. With a clipper bow and bowsprit, square stern and ports, a tall slender funnel, and side-lever engines by Robert Napier she was typical of her period. She was reboiled in 1846 and disposed of in 1851.

Now an exciting era ensued on the station with the St. George and Mona's Isle companies in direct competition and Captain Gill for the 'home side' commanding *Mona's Isle* competing against Lt. Tudor R.N. and the St. George's *Sophia Jane*. The first contest was on 16th August 1830; both vessels left Liverpool together and Captain Gill's *Mona's Isle* was beaten to Douglas by about 1½ minutes, but afterwards, this astute seaman usually got *Mona's Isle* to Douglas about forty minutes ahead of the opposition, the crossing being completed in about eight hours. A commercial battle was also joined and rates were slashed by both sides, but when the Liverpool company lowered its fare to 6d, the Manx Advertiser complained of the great number of mendicants coming to the island, this time the *Mona's Isle* company held

aloof from the contest. Then the St. George Company gave Lt. Tudor their large, fast *St. George* off the Irish station but Captain Gill maintained his reputation. The real and perpetual hazard however was the Irish Sea. Some two months after the racing started both vessels arrived at Douglas about the same time. Captain Gill, forseeing an inshore S.E. gale brewing, hastily put his passengers ashore, discharged his cargo and stood out to sea to ride out the storm, but Lt. Tudor anchored his *St. George*. During the night and at the height of the gale the *St. George* parted her cable and was swept onto the Conister Rock where she was dashed to pieces. Fortunately the crew were saved by the Douglas lifeboat, captained by Sir William Hillary founder of the Royal National Lifeboat Institution; his tomb is in St. George's churchyard, Douglas. Also in the churchyard may be seen the graves of victims of the dreadful cholera epidemic which afflicted Douglas in 1832, ironically the same year in which Sir William was instrumental in having erected on the Conister Rock the Tower of Refuge in which shipwrecked sailors might gain a respite.

Although the St. George Company put their *Orinoco* and *Prince Llewelyn* on the service they had lost heart and abandoned the station in July 1831. In July 1832, the Mona's Isle Company changed its name to the Isle of Man United Steam Packet Company and acquired another vessel P.S. *Mona*, which remained in service for nine years. Another purchase was P.S. *Queen of the Isle*, of 350 gross tons she was sold within ten years and after removal of her engines (they were fitted to the *Ben-my-Chree* of 1845) converted for her new owners to a barque-rigged sailing ship, evidence that the hull form of early steamers stuck closely to recognized norms.

In July 1835 the company adopted the title The Isle of Man Steam Packet Company, synonymous to generations of holidaymakers with the destination of their annual 'Wakes Week' break from the mills of Lancashire and Yorkshire. The Isle of Man Steam Packet Co. Ltd., was incorporated in the island on 3rd March 1885, and over the years the colourful and fascinating story of this famous shipping line has been thoroughly chronicled by maritime historians.

Douglas Station. c.1905. A busy mid-summer scene, the clock in the gabled gateway, with its oriental styled domes on the Peel Road corner (left) showing 11.35am in our time-warp. Although more improvements would follow, this was even at that time an imposing terminal for a narrow gauge railway, and a vast advance on the small wooden affair at the foot of Bank Hill that served the purpose when the line opened in 1873.

Much of Douglas station stands on a site reclaimed from tidal flats, although a timber yard on firmer ground occupied the site of what became the forecourt, and a saw-mill stood where the station buildings were to rise. The old harbour was near Bank Hill and the upper yards and masts of a sailing vessel appear over the roof-tops beyond the exit where a sign invites travellers to the 'STATION BAR'. In 1890, the laborious job of marshalling rakes of four-wheeled carriages was eased by modifying the couplings and buffers of the vehicles so that they could work close-coupled in pairs. Such a set is seen on the right, complete with roof mounted holders for the oil lamps.

Photo: Lens of Sutton.

St John's. 21st September 1962. Jimmy Kneale brings the ex County Donegal Railcars gently over the level crossing as Stationmaster the late George Crellin waits to collect the staff from Jack Watterson, acting as Guard. The wooden rustic style station buildings, protected by a crush rail were, in their green and cream livery ideally suited to this most salubrious of locations- the Central Hotel in the rear with its **'Bass'** advertisements was conveniently located for thirsty photographers. *Norman Jones.*

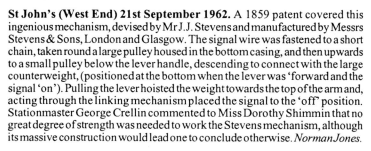

St John's (West End) 21st September 1962. A 1859 patent covered this ingenious mechanism, devised by Mr J.J. Stevens and manufactured by Messrs Stevens & Sons, London and Glasgow. The signal wire was fastened to a short chain, taken round a large pulley housed in the bottom casing, and then upwards to a small pulley below the lever handle, descending to connect with the large counterweight, (positioned at the bottom when the lever was 'forward and the signal 'on'). Pulling the lever hoisted the weight towards the top of the arm and, acting through the linking mechanism placed the signal to the 'off' position. Stationmaster George Crellin commented to Miss Dorothy Shimmin that no great degree of strength was needed to work the Stevens mechanism, although its massive construction would lead one to conclude otherwise. *Norman Jones.*

Port Erin. Summer 1967. The elegant awning complementing the double gabled brick station buildings looked very smart following general refurbishment and painting during the 'honeymoon' period of the Marquess of Ailsa's lease of the Isle of Man Railway. In the formative years Peel station was rather a paltry affair, but there was a complete re-vamping during 1902 - 1904 (completed just after the holiday season started), when not only the ornate buildings with their 'mock' timber framing and spiky finials were erected, but a platform was also provided, together with a new loco shed and goods shed and, the following year, a new warehouse. *Jean, John & Amy Lawless.*

St John's. 18th July 1962. Somnolence at St John's as Jimmy Kneale, at the controls of the ex County Donegal railcars awaits departure time, (4.39 pm) with the 4.30 pm from Peel booked Douglas (a 5.05 pm). By the crossing gates Mrs Crellin who seems to be in charge today chats to the solitary passenger who has alighted, whilst my colleagues the late Herbert Woodward and the Tourist Board's Jack Cretney are just visible taking some 'continuity' footage with the cine equipment at the far end of the platform. *Norman Jones.*

St John's 18th July 1962. The ubiquitous No.10. *G.H.Wood*, enters the junction station with an afternoon train from Peel, whilst my film crew record its arrival from the island platform. At the further (eastern) end of the unoccupied Ramsey line stands the Up M.N.Rly Starting Signal, No.8 and beyond that the obverse (with two arms on one post) side of No.s 2 and 3, the Peel Junction Signal and Ramsey Junction Signal respectively. To their right can be discerned the water supply tank, the long corrugated-iron Carriage Shed is to the left of Signal No.8 but the Signal Cabin cannot be seen at this range. *Norman Jones.*

Douglas Station.c.1905. The platform is clear, a lady with beribboned bonnet sits by the window in the waiting room (centre). To the right of the door a uniformed figure slouches in an attitude of despondency, head bowed, hands clasped; a weary member of the station staff recovering from the rush? Beyond the buffer stops we can now see the exit gate and picket fence, also the sailing packet's upper yard arms, and enamel signs extolling the use of 'Lifebuoy' Toilet Soap, and 'Hovis'. Two porters are preparing to deal with a heap of packages, the 'cabin' trunk and 'tin' box are typical containers of the day. The sleeved waistcoats were useful and obligatory items of apparel for many grades of railway staff everywhere, but these chaps must have been working as goods porters some time earlier, their trouser legs are covered with dust. *Lens of Sutton*

The Boom Years. The Isle Of Man Railway.

Moving around inland was difficult, roads being, to say the least inadequate. Transport was by horse-drawn vehicles and consequently the majority of visitors were concentrated mainly around Douglas. The island desperately required a railway system.

Schemes had been proposed from the middle of the nineteenth century onwards, but capital was scarce, and it was not until July 1873 that the 11½ mile long Douglas - Peel line of the Isle of Man Railway Co. was opened by the Duke of Sutherland when locomotive No.1, bearing the ducal name, drew the first train.

Sutherland was one of three engines (the first in Britain to have the much lauded pony trucks) which Messrs. Beyer, Peacock & Co., built for the Manx line. The sporty, steeply inclined cylinders, were 11ins diameter by 18ins stroke. Perhaps their crowning glory was a great, bell-mouthed dome, complete with Salter spring-balance safety valves, surmounting a small boiler about 2ft 10¾ins in diameter. With a working pressure of 120 lbs p.s.i. and coupled wheels 3ft 9ins diameter the Tractive Effort of this class of 2-4-0 locomotive at 85% boiler pressure was calculated as 4,940lbs. The coal supply was carried in a bunker inside the cab and the first engines, No.1 *Sutherland*, No.2 *Derby* and No.3 *Pender* each weighed (as built) about 17T 12cwts in working order. When later rebuilt with larger boilers and tanks with increased water capacity, the weight was increased to 20T 10cwts. The Isle of Man Railway Company remained faithful to Messrs. Beyer, Peacock and the 2-4-0T design and subsequent locomotives differed in detail alterations and dimensions only.

The Port Erin line was opened on 1st August 1874, when the company owned 27 route miles, 5 locomotives and about 40 assorted vehicles. By 1928 the route comprised 46¼ track miles, with 16 locomotives in service, 118 (mostly bogie) passenger vehicles and 151 assorted wagons and vans.

Whilst the southern portion of the island now enjoyed the benefits of a railway system the north-eastern sector, centred around Ramsey, a port and burgeoning seaside resort, remained isolated. This rather genteel town, which was proud to have been honoured by a Royal visit from Queen Victoria and Prince Albert in 1847, and dubbed itself 'Royal Ramsey' following a visit in 1902 by King Edward VII and Queen Alexandra, approached the Douglas based I.O.M. Rly with a view to joining the railway system. The I.O.M.

Railway Co. Directors were unwilling to fund a line which because of the terrain would be unable to follow a direct route along the eastern side of the island to Ramsey, whilst alternative routes would be through sparsely populated areas, unlikely to generate much traffic.

Nevertheless the people of Ramsey were not to be thwarted. An independent company was formed on 27th March 1877 and the Manx Northern Railway Company was authorized by a Manx Government Railway Act of 22nd March 1878. The capital was to be £90,000, with loans of a further £40,000 of which the Manx Government guaranteed a dividend of 4% on £25,000 of the preference capital for a period of twenty-five years from the date of the opening.

The line was to be constructed from Ramsey to a point near St. John's station on the Douglas-Peel line of the Isle of Man Railway, where a junction would be made, for which the Manx Northern Company would pay. Two routes were considered, both of which would terminate at St. John's. The route chosen was from Ramsey towards the western coastline via Lezayre, Sulby Bridge, Sulby Glen and Ballaugh to Bishop's Court. From Kirkmichael the line took a spectacular route along the cliffs, (the other path surveyed would have taken a more inland route) and quite spectacular viaducts were flung across Glen Wyllin, and Glen Mooar whilst the rails at Gob-y-Deigan (Devil's Mouth) were very near to the seaward edge of the cliff. At St. Germains however, the line turned inland, towards Peel Road and the junction at St. John's.

The line, 16½ miles long and to the same 3ft gauge as the Isle of Man Railway was opened on the 23rd September 1879, and a tramway from Ramsey to and along the quay at the harbour to facilitate the working of freight traffic was also provided for by the enabling Act. Provision had been made for the Head Office to be based in the station buildings at Ramsey, but a Douglas Office was set up instead, before the line opened.

The two companies were on good terms from the outset, the Manx Northern officials apparently receiving paternal advice from Mr G.H. Wood, Secretary and Manager of the Isle of Man Railway, and through coaches were soon working between Douglas and Ramsey.

The Manx Northern's first locomotives No.1. and No.2. (later named *Ramsey* and *Northern* although of a similar wheel notation to the I.O.M. Rly tud, differed in having cylinders which although placed outside were not inclined but horizontal, giving them a 'staid' appearance. Built by another famous firm of Manchester locomotive engineers Messrs. Sharp Stewart & Co., (formerly Sharp, Roberts & Co., and Sharp Brothers) they wore a smart Tuscan red livery. However, for their No.**3**. *Thornhill*, the Manx Northern ordered from Messrs. Beyer, Peacock at Gorton a locomotive to the I.O.M. Rly 's design.

The Isle of Man Railway's directors took exception to proposals in 1882 for a third railway. This, in the centre of the island, was promoted mainly by Charles Forman, a Civil Engineer from Glasgow. After various disputations a (new) Bill was introduced into the legislative assembly, The House of Keys in May 1883, and passed on the 13th June 1883, and the Foxdale Railway Co., Ltd., was soon up and running.

Foxdale, near St.John's, is (today) a pretty village on the bank of a tributary of the river Neb. At Lower Foxdale is the Hamilton Fall and this is the derivation of the name which does not relate to Vulpes vulpes (the Red Fox). Until quite recently there were no foxes on the island, (nor toads, newts, snakes, moles etc) the indigenous population is thought to have perished in the glacial epoch. In post-glacial times none of these species would appear to have crossed the land-bridge before it subsided beneath the sea, or were unable to survive if they did. The Scandinavian word for waterfall is 'Foss' and for a valley 'Dal' hence Foxdale.

Mining on the Isle of Man is thought to have commenced in the area of North and South Bradda (Port Erin) around the 13th century A.D. but it was to serve the busy local mines that the Foxdale railway was built. Mining seemed to be booming, and the Manx Northern was so impressed as to lease the Foxdale Railway for a period of fifty years from 5th January 1885. Unfortunately there was to be a general down-turn in mining in the British Isles following the discovery of vast deposits of ores overseas and the leasing arrangements led to financial disaster.

However in their day the mines were extensive, at one time 350 men were employed in the workings. Small wonder that Manx Northern tickets in the author's collection show bookings from Foxdale to stations throughout the island and I.O.M. Rly 'workman's returns' to St.John's ("all change for Foxdale Mines".)

Surface mining had started around Foxdale in the 1700's but in the third decade of the last century, the Isle of Man Mining Company was in control, their men extracting lead ores which also had a silver content. Notable shafts were Beckwith's 320 fathoms, Bawden's, which eventually reached over 250 fathoms, and Potts', also of considerable depth and, of course, radiating from these shafts underground, would be a warren of galleries and levels whilst above ground were the acres of washing floors, pumping gear, stationary engines, pit-head gears, spoil heaps etc

Trains began to run on the new line in 1886 and on Monday the 16th August a special train took shareholders to Foxdale, where the Isle of Man Mining Co., treated them to a sumptuous lunch, hosted by Captain Kitto, its principal, his title not being nautical but stemming from Cornish mining terminology. The bubble burst in the April of 1911 when the Mining Company went into voluntary liquidation.

Trains going to Foxdale faced a gradient of 1 in 49 (to be precise 48.6) with a short stretch of 1 in 12 to the workings and to cope with the heavy traffic expected, the Manx Northern purchased another, and much larger tank engine, No.**4** *Caledonia* was an 0-6-0T (six-coupled) with an 11ft wheelbase weighing 27 Tons in working order. As Works No.2178 it was built by Messrs. Dübs & Co., in 1885 at Glasgow. This was also the home of Mr Forman, prominent in Foxdale Railway affairs.

But traffic was dwindling and there was little heavy work for Caledonia to do and by the turn of the century the Manx Northern Railway, drained by its Foxdale venture, was in real trouble, and together with the Foxdale branch was absorbed by the Isle of Man Railway Co., in 1904, although the official transfer of ownership did not take place until 1905.

Today the track-bed of the Foxdale line has become a pleasant walk, and exploration of the area rewarding for the industrial archeologist, railway enthusiast and ordinary tourist alike.

Douglas. 28th July 1962. With the handsome awnings reaching to infinity, the 'Main Line Terminal' aspect of Douglas Station is heightened by the presence on Platform No.6. of a G.P.O. van, effecting a transfer of traffic between road and rail. Worthy of regard is the composite bogie carriage which contains a Guard's and Luggage Compartment - F43, one of the small series comprising Nos. F40-44, purchased from the Metropolitan Carriage & Wagon Co., (No.F43 in 1909) as a consequence of the need to replace the old Cleminson six-wheelers of the Manx Northern Railway Company (taken over in 1904) which were past their best.

This small class of 5 vehicles were, from new, fitted with electric lighting on Stone's Duplex system, although they were not the first so equipped, many of the older carriages having been converted from the smelly and inconvenient 'rape oil' lamps, already. *Photo: J.H. Price MCIT.*

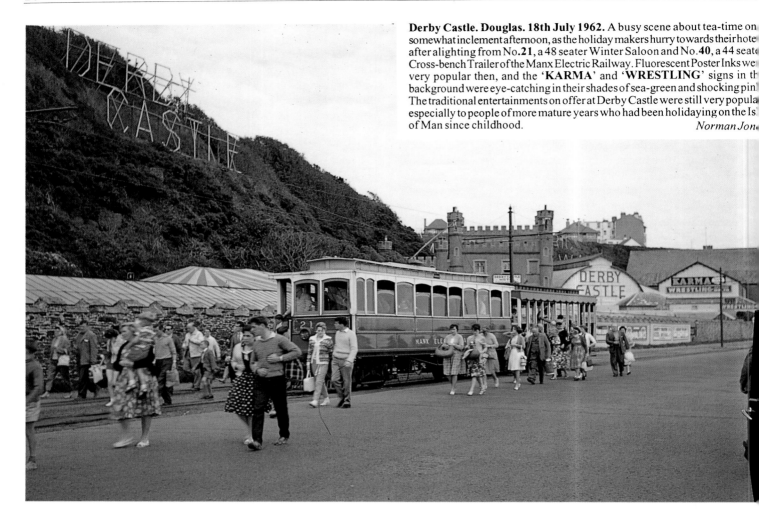

Derby Castle. Douglas. 18th July 1962. A busy scene about tea-time on [a] somewhat inclement afternoon, as the holiday makers hurry towards their hotel[s] after alighting from No.**21**, a 48 seater Winter Saloon and No.**40**, a 44 seate[r] Cross-bench Trailer of the Manx Electric Railway. Fluorescent Poster Inks we[re] very popular then, and the '**KARMA**' and '**WRESTLING**' signs in th[e] background were eye-catching in their shades of sea-green and shocking pin[k.] The traditional entertainments on offer at Derby Castle were still very popula[r,] especially to people of more mature years who had been holidaying on the Is[le] of Man since childhood.   *Norman Jon[es]*

Derby Castle Queens Promenade. October 1977. In this "Manx Year of Railways", acclaiming the Centenary of the M.E.R. and the resurgence of the Isle of Man Steam and Groudle Glen Railways, it is fitting that M.E.R. cars No's **6** and **22** should grace our final page of colour. No.**22** stands beside the Great Canopy, a handsome cast and wrought iron structure erected in 1896 and demolished in 1980. "Winter Saloon" No.**22** was one of four cars built in 1899 for the Ramsey Extension. This particular vehicle was almost destroyed by fire in September 1990 but a splendid replica was returned to service on 13th May 1992. No.**6** is one of a small batch of cars dating from 1894, known as "Tunnel" cars. As built, they had two front "sash" type windows, the modification to a one piece window being carried out in 1966. The passing Allegro car lends its own nostalgic touch as does the facade of hotels lining the graceful curve of the promenade that were a "home from home" for generations of holidaymakers.
W.G. Rear.

he Foxdale line, which began at a junction facing Ramsey on the Manx
orthern line, had its own small station on the south side, consisting of a
latform and red-brick building latterly occupied by the I.O.M. Railway's
ationmaster at St.John's. Climbing on a continuous gradient the Foxdale
ne swung round and crossed the I.O.M. Rly lines at the eastern (Douglas)
nd of St.John's by means of an overbridge, then running beneath the slopes
f Slieau Whallian (1,094) feet, the Halt at Waterfall was reached at 1½
iles another mile bringing trains to the Foxdale terminus. An average
urney time was about 15 minutes. Trains were usually 'mixed' and traffic
as so light after the I.O.M. Rly took over that one coach was sufficient to
andle the sparse number of passenger bookings. The 'regular' Foxdale
ach F39 is still in existence. By 1930 there were three trains (return) on
eekdays but traffic continually declined and by 1942 Isle of Man Road
ervice buses operated by the I.O.M. Railway Co. had taken over the route.
aledonia's weight and long wheelbase made her something of a liability,
t she was loaned to the contractors building the Snaefell Mountain
ailway and when during World War I a prisoner of war or detention camp
as set up at Knockaloe near Peel and served by a (long lifted) branch this
came a regular duty for Caledonia. Her weight was also an advantage
ring any severe winter weather when, fitted with a snow-plough she could
e seen clearing the drifts that at times blocked cuttings on the lines to Port
in and Ramsey.

In the years immediately prior to the last war (Hitler's) there was a demand
for slag and spoil from the disused mines, this traffic passing mainly in the
winter, and in two seasons over 50,000 tons of waste was taken to Douglas
by rail for building site development. As hostilities with Nazi Germany
hotted up this material was also used in constructing runways on the island
for the R.A.F. Once again *Caledonia* came into her own taking charge of the
spoil trains.

In 1940, due to the absence of holidaymakers following the outbreak of war,
the I.O.M. Rly's passenger receipts fell by £12,690 and the Manx Government was asked to make up the short-fall in revenue with a similar scheme
to that by which Westminster guaranteed Britain's 'Big-Four' a nett revenue
based on their average 1935/6/7 profits.

Just before the war started the I.O.M. Railway's route mileage was 46¼ over
which a yearly average of about 775,000 passengers and 56,000 tons of
freight were carried.

On the matter of 'named trains' the "Cock o' the North" and "Port Erin
Flyer" were noteworthy, and presented an impressive spectacle of steam
on the narrow gauge as they left Douglas Station simultaneously at 10.05am,
every weekday morning in the holiday season. Invariably the engine of the
"Flyer" would be 'blowing off', needing every ounce of steam for the 3 mile
climb at 1 in 65/70 to Port Soderick.

When first introduced this Port Erin train performed a non-stop run, but later

len Wyllin. c.1935. Oblivious to all but the
otographer, a small group pose unconcern-
lly whilst a train trundles sedately across the
aduct some fifty feet above their heads. A
art waitress in starched cap and apron stands
the rear of the party, but one wonders about
e more prominent uniformed figure, thumbs
waistcoat pockets, could he be a 'charabanc
iver' or a member of the I.O.M.Rly staff? The
trance to the Glen was only a few minutes
alk by a footpath from Kirkmichael station, to
nich special excursions were run from Doug-
s and Ramsey. A special siding was laid in to
commodate the empty stock. In 1935 the Isle
Man Railway bought the Glen and improved
natural attractions by setting up swings and
undabouts, laying bowling greens and install-
g a boating lake, but our photograph seems to
e-date these features.   *Lens of Sutton.*

GLEN WYLLIN. I.O.M.

[left]
Douglas. c.1904. Douglas Corporation's Cable
Car No. 75 stands at the Victoria Street terminus,
about mid-day judging by the shortness of the cast
shadows, and a sweltering mid-summer day at that,
with ladies shaded by picture hats making their way
to the covered toast-rack horse car. The route
names painted on the valance of No. 75 are Victoria
Street, Woodbourne Road, Ballaquayle Road. The
name 'blacked out' would have been Broadway,
confirming that our photographer was active after
January 1902 when the section of the cable car
route down Broadway towards the promenade was
abandoned. We must also admire the fine sweep of
promenade, the Loch being linked to the Central by
the Harris Promenade and in the distance, leading
towards the tramway termini, the Queens
Promenade.   *Photo: Lens of Sutton.*

a stop was inserted in the schedule at Port St. Mary. Nevertheless the journey time for the 15½ mile trip was only 40 minutes (37 minutes to Port St. Mary) and on a good day 800 passengers might entrain, reference to bus timetables of the period indicates that the journey might take 70 minutes by road.

The "Cock o' the North" for Ramsey was booked to cover the 25 miles in 60 minutes (75 minutes by stopping trains, 70 minutes by motor bus). There was a stop at St. John's to detach a Peel portion, and at Kirkmichael where a Ramsey-Douglas train was crossed. Some fine running took place and Mr D.S. Barrie, a knowledgeable and esteemed writer of the period mentioned a run with No.13 *Kissack*, hauling a 45 ton train which was timed over a mile to average 41 m.p.h. with a maximum of 45 m.p.h. No wonder the running of the "Cock o' the North" could be performed in even time, excluding standing time at eight intermediate stops.

As the volume of traffic grew more locomotives came from Gorton, No.13 *Kissack* of 1910 ending the sequence until 1926 when a much larger engine, but still of the same basic design arrived. In the 1920's very heavy trains hauled by two or even three of the older engines were worked between Douglas and Port Erin, whilst special 'Boat Trains' were also rostered. With such heavy loadings in mind No.16 *Mannin*, with a Tractive Effort of 8,810 lbs, was ordered.

The non-standard Manx Northern engines, No.1 *Ramsey* and No.2 *Northern* were not used intensively and fell into the 'standby' category. No.2 was scrapped in 1912 and the fate of No.1, which disappeared from the stage

c.1918, is uncertain. The M.N.R.'s Beyer, Peacock No.3 *Thornhill*, name after the home of the M.N.R. Chairman, worked alongside its I.O.M. R compatriots after the merger, renumbered as I.O.M. Rly No.14 but retaini its 'given' name.

In 1930 the fleet comprised:

No.	Name	Built	Makers No.
No.1	*Sutherland*	Built 1873	Makers No.125?
No.2	*Derby*	Built 1873	Makers No.125?
No.3	*Pender*	Built 1873	Makers No.125?
No.4	*Loch*	Built 1874	Makers No.141?
No.5	*Mona*	Built 1874	Makers No.141?
No.6	*Peveril*	Built 1875	Makers No.152?
No.7	*Tynwald*	Built 1880	Makers No.2038
No.8	*Fenella*	Built 1894	Makers No.361?
No.9	*Douglas*	Built 1896	Makers No.381?
No.10	*G.H.Wood*	Built 1905	Makers No.466?
No.11	*Maitland*	Built 1905	Makers No.466?
No.12	*Hutchinson*	Built 1908	Makers No.512?
No.13	*Kissack*	Built 1910	Makers No.538?
No.14	*Thornhill*	Built 1880	Makers No.2028
No.15	*Caledonia*	Built 1885	Makers No.217?
No.16	*Mannin*	Built 1926	Makers No.629?

Douglas - Sea Front. c.1960. Truly an evocation of the seaside holiday of golden childhood is encapsulated in this view of the lovely horseshoe swee of Douglas Bay, curving round towards that focal point for so many visitors, the legendary Derby Castle site, with its varied entertainments, the Man Electric Railway terminus, and the cast iron magnificence of the Great Canopy which sheltered the waiting horse trams. The canopy was built by the Isl of Man Tramways & Electric Power Co., in 1896 and demolished, following a shock announcement that it was unsafe, in 1980. In their almost immort fashion, the horse trams link the steamer piers and electric railway, the notice on the dash declaiming 'ALL THE WAY 8d' 'STAGE 5d' i.e. 3.33p an 2.08p respectively. Advertisements for Jacobs Biscuits and the Villa Marina have stood the test of time, but how fashions have changed since we looke at picture the of Cable Car No.75. We have short skirts and frothy blouses for the girls, short sleeves and casual dress for the lads, but there are still rowin boats on a calm sea, and packed beaches, and in the 'Golden 60's' there was scant apprehension concerning polluted seaweed or beaches that were le than immaculate, most folk expecting Mother Nature and her tides to take care of that.   *Photo: Isle of Man Tourist Boar*

Miniature Railway, Groudle Glen, Isle of Man

Groudle Glen. Lhen Coan Station c.1900. The literal translation of Lhen Coan is 'lovely Glen', even more apt nowadays when the area has become so richly afforested. Shown to advantage in this scene, is the smart pavilion style black and white gabled station building cum carriage shed which, with its tiled awning was still extant when I visited Groudle in 1962 and survived until demolished in the 1970's. The 2-4-0T Bagnall locomotive looks a picture with highly polished chimney cap and dome: the locomotive service and inspection pit are seen in the right-hand corner of the view. The engine livery at this time was dark green with gold lining, and the stretchers of the smoke box door hinges, and the securing handles, have been burnished until the bare steel shines like silver. The preponderance of straw 'boaters' indicates not only the male fashion of the period but a blisteringly hot summer day, which has proved overpowering for the seated figure on the left who has pushed his bowler hat on to the back of his head and is engrossed in his (Sunday?) paper. Worthy of scrutiny and speculation are the two figures (near right) in conversation, the closest figure uniformed, both carrying that other mark of the well dressed man, a walking stick: the official looking bowler hatted gentleman has his eye on the camera. *Lens of Sutton.*

GROUDLE

DERBY CASTLE to GROUDLE

Manx Electric Railway
Available ... ... Journey.
Must be ... ... inspection
and given ... ... Issued
subject to Company ... e-laws.

GROUDLE to DERBY CASTLE

Return Journey
Williamson, Printer, Ashton

A 5330

St. John's. 19th May 1956. This crisp shot, looking eastwards towards Douglas not only makes a charming picture but features prominently the æsthetic appeal of the bridge which carried the Foxdale line across the route of the Isle of Man Railway by means of a masonry and brick arched structure that had a span of 25 ft and a height of 11 ft 9 ins. to the crown of the arch. The facing connection operated by the ground-lever adjacent to the neatly capped bridge abutment leads to the abandoned gravel siding - on the south side of the line - from which ballast was at one time obtained. Within its confines are observed two derelict **M** class wagons and the remains of a conveyor and other equipment, whilst beyond the gravel pit is the Down Distant Signal. The next level crossing to be traversed by a Douglas bound train would be at Ballacraine - 1½ miles from St. John's - and there was once a halt here which it was hoped would be patronised by visitors to Glen Helen, an attraction then being promoted, but of which expectations were not realised, the stop being abandoned. *Photo: J. H. Price MCIT.*

ISLE OF MAN RAILWAY

NOTICE.—The hours or times stated in the Company's Time Tables, Books, Bills and Notices are appointed as those at which it is intended so far as circumstances will permit, that the trains shall depart from and arrive at the several Stations, but their departure or arrival at the times stated is not guaranteed, nor will the Company under any circumstances be held responsible for delay or detention, however occasioned, or any consequences arising therefrom. The right to stop the trains at any Station on the lines, although not marked as a stopping Station, and to alter or suspend the running of any of the trains, is reserved.

This Time Table will Not Operate on Any Day that may require a Special Time Table.

Time Table for Monday, 21st May, 1956, and until further notice

DOUGLAS—PORT ERIN LINE — WEEKDAYS | SUNDAYS

To PORT ERIN

Stations		6		8		10		12		14		16		18		2	
DOUGLAS Dep.	...	10 10	Runs from 2nd July	10 40		11 50		2 15		3 10		4 15		5 25	Runs from 2nd July	2 30	Runs from 8th July
Port Soderick ... ,,	...			10 51		12 1		2 26		3 21		4 26		5 36		2 41	
Santon ... ,,	...					R		2 34		R		R		R			
Ballasalla ... ,,	...			11 7		12 17		2 42		3 37		4 42		5 52		2 57	
Castletown ... ,,	...	10 40		11 13		12 23		2 48		3 43		4 48		5 58		3 3	
Colby ... ,,	...	10 47		R		R		R		R		4 56		6 6		3 11	
Port St. Mary ... ,	...	10 54		11 28		12 38		3 3		3 58		5 3		6 13		3 18	
PORT ERIN Arr.	...	10 56		11 30		12 40		3 5		4 0		5 5		6 15		3 20	

To DOUGLAS

	1		7		9		11		13		17		19		1	
PORT ERIN Dep.	7 10	...	10 40		11 55	Runs from 2nd July	1 0		2 0		4 20		5 30	Runs from 2nd July	4 25	Runs from 8th July
Port St. Mary ... ,,	7 13		10 43		11 58		1 3		2 3		4 23		5 33		4 28	
Colby ... ,,	7 18		10 48		12 3		1 8		2 8		4 28		5 38		4 33	
Castletown ... ,,	7 27		10 58		12 12		1 17		2 17		4 37		5 47		4 42	
Ballasalla ... ,,	7 33		11 8		12 18		1 23		2 23		4 43		5 53		4 48	
Santon ... ,,	7 42		R		R		R		2 33				R			
Port Soderick ... ,,	7 50		11 25		12 35						5 0		6 10		5 5	
DOUGLAS Arr.	8 0		11 35		12 45		1 50		2 50		5 10		6 20		5 15	

DOUGLAS—PEEL and RAMSEY LINES — WEEKDAYS | SUNDAYS

To PEEL AND RAMSEY

	2		4		10		12		14		16		18	20	B	
DOUGLAS Dep.			9 55		10 30		11 45		2 10		3 25		4 15	4 15		...
Union Mills ... ,,		Not after 19th July							R				4 22			
Crosby ... ,,			10 9		10 44		11 59	Runs from 20th July	2 24		3 39		4 29	4 29		...
St. John's Arr.			10 18		10 53		12 8		2 33		3 48		4 38	4 38		...
St. John's Dep.			10 21		10 56		12 14		2 36		3 51		4 41	4 41		...
PEEL Arr.			10 30		11 5		12 23		2 45		4 0		4 50	4 50		...
St. John's Dep.					10 58		12 13		2 38		3 53		...	4 41		
St. Germain's ... ,,											R					
Kirk Michael ,,	8 5				11 19		12 34		2 59		4 14		...	5 2	Runs from 20th July	
Ballaugh ... ,,	8 13				11 27		12 42		3 7		4 23	Not after 19th July	...	5 10		
Sulby Glen ... ,,	8 19				11 33		12 48		3 13		4 29		...	5 17		
Sulby Bridge ... ,,	8 22				11 36		12 51		3 16		R		...	5 20		
RAMSEY Arr.	8 31				11 45		1 0		3 25		4 40			5 30		

To DOUGLAS

	1		5		7		11		15		17		19	21		
RAMSEY Dep.	6 45	...			10 5		1 45				3 45		4 5	4 50		...
Sulby Bridge ... ,,	6 55				10 15		1 55				3 55		4 15	5 0		...
Sulby Glen ... ,,	6 58				10 18		1 58				3 58	Runs from 20th July	4 18	5 3		...
Ballaugh ... ,,	7 4				10 24		2 4				4 5		4 24	5 9		...
Kirk Michael ... ,,	7 12				10 32		2 12				4 15		4 32	5 17		...
St. Germain's ... ,,	R						R									
St. John's Arr.	7 32				10 52		2 32				4 37		4 52	5 37		...
PEEL Dep.	7 25		8 5	...	10 45	12 0	2 25		4 30		4 30		...			
St. John's Arr.	7 34		8 14		10 54	12 9	2 34		4 39		4 39		...			
St. John's Dep.	7 37		8 16		10 57		2 37		4 42		4 42	Not after 19th July	4 57	5 42		...
Crosby ... ,,	7 47		8 27		11 7		2 47		4 52		4 52		5 7	5 52		...
Union Mills ... ,,	7 54		8 34										5 14			
DOUGLAS Arr.	8 0		8 40		11 20		3 0		5 5	5 5			5 20	6 5		...

R — Request stop.

See Bus Time Table for evening services from Douglas in connection with steamer.

B —SUNDAY MORNINGS, commencing 8th July — TRAINS to KIRK BRADDAN — Douglas depart 10-10 a.m., 10-40 a.m., returning after the Open-air Church Service.

Town Bus Service operates between Pier Arcade and Douglas Station in connection with boat trains.

The Route & Stations Described.c.1955.

Douglas Station of the 1950's, some ten minutes walk from the steamer, was a splendidly ornate building enhanced by a forecourt and imposing clock tower whilst the entrance to the circulating area was surmounted by an elegant glazed canopy. Passing beneath this the thirsty traveller could head for the welcoming and licenced refreshment rooms. The spacious circulating area was also glazed and, sheltered beneath handsome awnings stood the two long island platforms, trains for Peel and Ramsey being joined at that on the right, although in later years the Ramsey section might be found marshalled beside the (inner) face of this northern platform; it would be drawn out and joined up with the Peel section for the run to St. John's where the Peel and Ramsey lines diverged. Port Erin traffic used either face of the other (southern) platform. The goods yard and a large carriage shed are located on the south side of the station, that is the left-hand side as one enters. The signal box is on the same side, whist the locomotive shed and works then as now are across the tracks on the northern side.

Let us visualise the routes in their guise of this period.

On their exit from Douglas, the Peel and Port Erin lines run parallel for a short distance until their ways part after crossing the "Nunnery" girder bridge spanning the river Glass. The Peel line then follows the course of the River Dhoo (hence Douglas) westward on rising gradients, passing the small wooden booking hut at Braddan Halt, (used on Sundays for holiday-makers enjoying the regular excursion to the popular open-air religious services held at Kirk Braddan). Then on to Union Mills (2½ m). Union Mills has two curved platforms and is decidedly attractive, with the wooden buildings on

the right painted in cream and green. At the time of my visit, it was mainly a request stop in the Down direction. Still following the gentle curves of the river the line continues via Closemoar Level Crossing to Crosby (4¾m), a crossing place, with a platform on the right, a siding and small corrugated iron goods shed. The line then climbs for about two miles, before descending to St.John's (8½m), where the train may halt at the junction (eastern end) before entering the station. The only other signal box on the system (besides Douglas) is located at St.John's.

In the case of Peel/Ramsey trains which left Douglas combined, the train is divided here, the Peel portion is then drawn into the station by the train engine, whilst a waiting locomotive couples onto the vehicles for Ramsey and brings them forward on the appropriate line.

A low gravel covered island platform stands between the Peel and Ramsey loops, and there is another platform on the south side on which are found an attractive wooden booking office and all necessary passenger facilities. The buildings are painted in colours of cream and green. A water tank is situated at the eastern end of the junction as is a large carriage shed. Trains from Douglas enter St.John's beneath the bridge which carried the Foxdale Branch over the main line at this the eastern end of the layout, details of that branch having already been mentioned in the section entitled *The Boom Years*

The Kirkmichael-Castletown road via Foxdale obstructed the railway by the level crossing at the western end of St.John's and over this the Peel and Ramsey lines ran parallel, continuing so until the Peel line bore away to the

Douglas Station. 10th August 1963. Douglas Station Clock Tower and pedestrian entrance to Forecourt. What a wealth of memories this superbly detailed photograph recreates, of Manx holidays in the 'flower-power' years. Could any parent resist being so inveigled into Mr Risdale's crowded emporium where an amazing collection of beach balls, spades, buckets and other indispensable elements of a day on the beach opened the most tightly knotted of purse strings. The two identically jersied boys on the kerbside with their mum, the smaller boy clutching his new treasures with both arms, will be now en-route to the sea front. And what a wonderful medley of newspapers, picture-postcards and advertising placards are on display, whilst the posters on the upper windows remind passers-by that TOILET REQUISITES AND PROPRIETARY MEDICINES are sold as well as KODAK FILM. Note, too, that those who wished could 'smoke themselves silly' without qualm on TOM THUMB CIGARS, WOODBINES (the great little cigarette - popularly called 'gaspers') not forgetting CAPSTAN, PLAYERS and many other long forgotten brands then to be found on any tobacconist or newsagent's shelves. And what a handsome piece of period work the fine entrance arch is, the handsome clock in its pedimented tower flanked by the fine gilded domes, whilst the intricate tracery of the wrought iron gates is well matched to the theme of this stunning entrance, a nice - if orthodox touch - is added by the massive 'grecian' urns adorning the caps of the brick piers. A varied display of large and small posters advertise the excellent value of the 'Run-About Ticket' which was only 12/6 (62.5p) in those pre-decimal days, whilst a smaller bill offers a 1/- (5p) fare to Kirk Braddan.   *Photo: G. Biddle.*

left after crossing the river Neb, and then traversing a stretch of rolling countryside descended on a falling gradient of 1 in 80 to follow the river in a narrow valley to arrive at Peel (terminus 11½m). The station's island platform is adjacent to the harbour, a lively scene with its array of small boats moored at the quays; there is also a splendid view of Peel Hill, the Castle and St.Germain's Cathedral. The terminus at Peel (11½ m) is approached over the gated Mill Street crossing, beside which, on the left, stands the engine shed and water tank. The pavillion like station buildings are at the end of the long island platform, the goods yard, with shed, cattle and goods platforms are on the right, and on the harbour side a carriage siding and engine run-round lines.

Reverting to the Ramsey line. This turned away from the Peel line to run north-west on a rising gradient of 1 in 132, partly through cuttings to Peel Road Halt (Poortown) and St.Germains (2⁷/₈m).

For about three miles from White Strand beach the line pursues a coastal path, then descends at about 1 in 100 to cross the fine viaducts at Glen Mooar and Glen Wyllin. The Isle of Man Railway Co. purchased the Glen Wyllin pleasure grounds in 1935. And so to Kirkmichael (7¼m). There is no platform but substantial stone station buildings. The line swings east across rolling farmland passing the private halt at Bishop's Court and over Orrisdale Nos. 1 and 2 level crossings to Ballaugh (10¹/₈m) which has a crossing loop, like the previous two stations.

The line continues, skirting the mountains to reach Sulby Glen (12¼m). This is quite an impressive little station, with level crossing, a platform and buildings enhanced by an awning, there is also a small goods siding. A run through the fields for another ¾ mile reveals one more crossing place as on descending gradients the closed Lezayre Station is passed and one arrives at Ramsey (16½m). As befits a terminus substantial stone buildings are found here, there is a bay line on the south side whilst, opposite are the corrugated-iron carriage shed, loco shed, livestock platform and goods sidings. The Harbour Branch rails were concreted over in 1954.

We return to Douglas to sample the Port Erin line journeying along the south-east route. It climbs sharply shortly after leaving Douglas through rocky cuttings, the sea then comes into view far below, and it is possible to glimpse the route of the former Douglas Head Marine Drive Tramway. Port Soderick is reached at 3¹/₈m. The platform is on the left of the line the two-storey station buildings opposite. Then comes a climb through a wooded valley and a steep (1 in 60 in parts) descent to Santon (5⁵/₈m). Santon, with its row of palm trees is rather reminiscent of the M.E.R's Laxey Station. The gradient is generally in favour of the engine now; on through hilly terrain and there is a glimpse of Ronaldsway Airport before arrival at Ballasalla (8³/₈m). This location is reputedly the haunt of the 'Little People' fairies, who will "ill-wish" you should you cross the road bridge without greeting them - the station has only rudimentary wooden buildings and lacks platforms. The line proceeds mostly then, in shallow cutting to arrive at Castletown (9⁷/₈m) with handsome, masonry built station buildings and goods shed. An overbridge takes the tracks across a stream and fairly open country to pass the site of the defunct Ballabeg Station and, climbing gradually reaches Colby (12¾m). The line descends to Port St.Mary (14¾m) where the platform is on the left and, excluding Douglas, the station buildings are some of the most impressive on the line. A short climb brings the journey to an end at Port Erin terminus (15³/₈m), its long island platform bisected by a roadway. The brick station buildings are at the terminal end, with engine and goods shed on the south side.

A Time of Change. The Post-War Years

It was evident long before the end of the 1950's that the availability and popularity of air travel and package holidays particularly based on Spanish and Mediterranean coasts and private car ownership was diverting holiday makers away from the long established resorts. It was also clear that the rising generation was looking for a different type of holiday and that the charm of the lovely Manx glens and coastline, the appeal and peace of an island where a splendid railway, bus and tramway system, enabled life to be enjoyed at a leisurely pace was not in itself enough to keep visitors coming at pre-war levels. Nevertheless the Isle of Man Railway kept going although obviously all was not well. In 1962 it was reported that Nos. 3, and 9 were in store awaiting re-boilering (although No.11 *Maitland* had received a boiler renewal during the winter of 1959/60). But careful management produced an operating surplus which rose by £2,887 to £12,350 for the year. Some track maintenance had been done and it was reported that locomotives Nos. 5, 8 and 12 had done the bulk of the work. Freight was worked over the Ramsey line 'as required' and as a cost reduction measure it was proposed that the ex County Donegal Railcars, purchased in 1961 and landed in the island on the 7th May that year, should work the traffic between Douglas and Peel during the summer season.

Regrettably traffic on the I.O.M. Rly continued to decline and by the end of 1964, the only regular working left was that between Douglas and Port Erin.

The Isle of Man Railway was re-opened throughout on 7th June 1965, and a new halt was built on the Ramsey line to serve the Curragh wild-life park but tourism was more than ever in the doldrums, even the road services suffered and were cut back, whilst all rail services ceased on 15th November 1965.

Manx people were shaken by the announcement on 20th January 1966 that the Isle of Man Railway would not reopen that year. In April 1967 a group of enthusiasts formed the MANX STEAM RAILWAY SOCIETY (later renamed ISLE OF MAN STEAM RAILWAY SUPPORTERS ASSOCIATION).and a Government (Transport) Commission decided that the steam railway was a tourist attraction and should be saved if possible. Nevertheless members of the preservation society faced problems exceeding those encountered by their counterparts on the mainland. The Isle of Man Railway was an integral part of the island's infrastructure, its proprietors also running a fleet of 'Red' stage-carriage buses and a road transport network, were understandably not inclined to give enthusiasts a free-hand. No trains ran in 1966, but the Commission had not been idle and the atmosphere was euphoric when it was announced on 1st March 1967 at Douglas that the Directors of the Isle of Man Railway Co. had agreed that the Marquess of Ailsa should lease the entire network for a period of 21 years commencing on 1st April 1967. The intention was to have part of the line open later in the summer.

Lord Ailsa was the Chairman of the new enterprise, the other directors were Lord Strange, Lt-Col.P.A.Spittall, M.H.K., Mr G.V.H.Kneale, M.H.K., and Sir Philip Wombwell, M.B.E. (ex Royal Engineers). Sir Philip who had worked on military railways in the Mediterranean theatre of war was to live on the island and become the line's General Manager.

The locomotives which required the least attention would be used, No.1 *Mona*, No.8 *Fenella*, No.10 *G.H.Wood*, No.11 *Maitland*, and No.12 *Hutchinson* whilst the 0-6-0T *Caledonia* could also be put into service if need be. It was hoped that the Douglas-St.John's-Peel line could be re-opened on the 3rd June to catch the best of the summer season's trade, and that to Port Erin the following year.

The new owners made an energetic start and it was hoped that their go-ahead policies might revitalise not only the steam railway, but the declining Manx tourist industry in general.

Mainland newspapers took little interest in the resurgence but railway journalists followed events closely. The railway's workshops were to rebuild suitable wagons to transport 8ft x 8ft containers and three former M.N.Rly six-wheel coaches would be converted into car-flats; 20 Ton tank wagons were also envisaged. No.**13**. *Kissack* and No.**16**. *Mannin* were to be reboilered during the winter and members of the Isle of Man Steam Railway Supporters Association would be invited to clean and paint stored locomotives for static display.

2nd June 1968 was a Gala day when, with all the atmosphere of a Victorian occasion a heavily loaded inaugural train left Douglas hauled by locomotive No.**12** *Hutchinson*, bound for Castletown and Port Erin, with No.**8** *Fenella* assisting in the rear up Port Soderick Bank. Trains were scheduled for all routes excepting the Foxdale Branch. On week-days three trains ran between Douglas and Peel, four between Douglas and Port Erin and one each

way Mondays, Wednesdays and Fridays between Douglas and Ramsey. No.**16** *Mannin,* No.**6** *Peveril,* No. **1** *Sutherland* and No.**14** *Thornhill* (the latter ex M.N. Rly and in that company's Tuscan Red livery) were on static display at St.Johns. The ex County Donegal railcars were to be slotted into the service at off-peak times and instead of running them coupled together it was proposed to work them as single units, which would entail making some arrangement to turn the single-ended units at Douglas and Peel.

During 1967 there were a few operating mishaps. On Monday, 21st August No.**10** *G.H. Wood* working the 12.20pm Douglas to Peel service over-ran the loop at the unstaffed halt of Union Mills. Whilst waiting for one of the train crew to hold over the weighted point-lever so that No.**10** could set back into the loop, the waiting train was struck head-on by No.**12** *Hutchinson* in charge of the 11.55am Peel to Douglas train. Three people were slightly injured and taken to hospital but not detained. The headstocks of both engines were quite

Douglas Station. 10th August 1963. Forsaking the Aladdin's Cave of Mr Risdale's establishment and descending through the triumphal arch to the station forecourt, the heraditaments fulfil any expectations that such an elaborate edifice might have aroused. The fine, red brick buildings present those idiosyncrasies of late 19th, early 20th century architecture which the 1930's originators of the concrete cubism style of that epoch would disdain, but which is becoming ever more appreciated as indicative of the ebullient and confident mood of what was an unparalleled period of growth and expansion. However, the expansion in tourism was declining markedly when our picture was taken and despite it being mid-summer only two ladies, their island holiday almost over, have alighted from the Peel train and with suitcases at their feet await the Douglas Corporation motor bus on the No.27 service. During the 'boom years' the fact that Douglas station was some distance from the steamer piers and horse tram terminus was of little moment, there was really no other way to travel and folk were used to walking anyway, but the lack of a connection certainly proved a negative factor in the post war years. One can only speculate on the outcome, had Mr Alexander Bruce's offer, through the medium of his Isle of Man Tramways & Electric Power Co as part of a package deal involving free lighting of part of the promenade, to both electrify the horse tramway system and build an extension line from its terminus, along the North Quay to Douglas Station, had been accepted. *Photo: G. Biddle.*

seriously damaged and needed replacement, whilst carriage No.F21 the leading coach on the 12.20pm sustained damage to an end compartment. One consequence of the accident was the cancellation of several trains as with the damaged locomotives taken out of service, only the railcars and three engines could be rostered for duty. Three days later No.11 *Maitland* was in trouble when working a return Ramsey excursion. It was a well loaded train comprised of carriages Nos. F29, F30 and F31, which left Douglas at 9.05pm. Union Mills was again the scene of the incident. No.11 took the wrong road on the facing points and carriage No.F30 was derailed. Fortunately there were no injuries this time and the passengers were taken home by bus. Clearance operations were postponed until the morning when trains were again cancelled whilst the coach was re-railed and the track re-instated. No.11 quite undamaged was hauled off to Peel where it was steamed up and then worked the 2.35pm train to Douglas.

With such a superb narrow-gauge, steam railway again fully operational one would have expected not only railway enthusiasts but tourists generally to hasten to sample the delights of this most scenic of lines. Sadly this was not so. With hind-sight it might be said better perhaps not to have re-opened

the entire network at once, but one would hardly anticipate such a lack lustre response and tardy support for such a bold enterprise.

Predictably, therefore, after running the railway for two years the Marquess re-negotiated his agreement with the Isle of Man Railway Co., subsequently giving up his island residence and returning to his Scottish home.

The summer of 1969 saw the registration of The Isle of Man Victorian Steam Railway Co., Ltd., its objective to work steam trains over the Douglas to Port Erin line. The Marquess of Ailsa was loath to see the railway go into terminal decline and agreed to visit the Isle of Man once a month to oversee the new venture, whilst day to day management would be in the hands of Mr Max Crookall, Treasurer of the Isle of Man Railway Supporters' Association. A Manx Government subsidy of £7,500 p.a. for three years would help toward the operating costs of a train service based on the Port Erin line.

Problems continued to assail the attempts to maintain a steam presence and it became a political issue. The Manx Department of Tourism became involved and the Marquess ran the Port Erin line for that body in the 1970-1 season but this marked the end of his participation and the I.O.M. Rly Co. resumed control.

Douglas.16th July 1962. Two signal boxes only were required on the Isle of Man's narrow gauge railway with this, at Douglas, being the larger of the two. The other was located at St.John's. 2-4-0T locomotive No.**8** *Fenella* is standing near to signals Nos. 26 and 27, controlling access to the long head shunt that leaves the Carriage Shed i.e. the long corrugated-iron building to the left of the signal box. The Port Erin line (south) and Peel line (north) operated as independent lines within station limits; the goods yard and carriage sidings were entered from the southernmost line and the locomotive shed and workshops from the north side, both of the latter buildings being on the extreme right of our photograph. The signal box contains a 36 lever frame by Messrs Dutton & Co., of Worcester, featuring their patent 'spring-handle' lever. In the case of the 'Dutton' lever, the handle is itself pivoted; it adopts a vertical position when pulled until the movement is completed and when the lever is moved to its limit of travel the handle is pushed forward to make the locking effective. Signalling and working practices on the Isle of Man Railway differed in some ways from those customary elsewhere, and the sequence of levers in Douglas Station Box was somewhat unusual.
                                                          Norman Jones

The I.O.M Railway in Travail

In April 1972 it was reported that the summer service operating from 29th May to 15th September would consist of four trains each way Mondays to Fridays between Douglas and Port Erin. The Isle of Man Railway gained some publicity when it was widely reported that during a visit to the Isle of Man in August 1972, Her Majesty the Queen, together with Prince Philip, Princess Anne and Prince Andrew would travel on a special Royal Train from Castletown to Douglas. The engine used no. **13** *Kissack* was adorned with five flags and a shield, the Royal Party rode in saloon carriage No. F36, which the Queen Mother had used during her 1963 visit. The Company Chairman Mr J.M. Cain and General Manager Mr William Lambden accompanied the Royal Visitors. Despite this event, passenger loadings were disappointing and although a Government grant of £12,000 was received, the shortfall during 1972/3 was more than twice that amount. The British Railways Board's consultancy firm Transmark, was called in; their report to the Manx Government in 1974 was discouraging for those fighting to keep the railway going. Nevertheless the I.O.M.Rly Co.s Chairman's report circulated with the Statement of Accounts & Balance Sheet for the Isle of Man Railway for 1975 remarked that due to the strength of its investments the year had been good financially. However the company would not work trains out of Douglas next season but over a short section of line between Ballasalla and Castletown, whilst arrangements would be made to sell by auction surplus stock and equipment.

In the March Mr Donald Shaw, the railway's Locomotive, Carriage & Wagon Superintendent for 53 years had retired, but he agreed to act as consultant for a shortened Ballasalla-Castletown-Port Erin line. Two societies were now adding their endeavours to keep the steam railway going. The Isle of Man Steam Railway Supporters Association and the Isle of Man Railway Society.

This was in the nature of a reprieve and in 1976 the trains ran between Ballasalla and Port Erin, stopping 'on request' at Castletown and Port St. Mary, their status reduced to that of unstaffed halts. Four trains ran each day Monday to Friday, between 16th May and 24th September.

The venture was definitely not a success, the isolated section of railway only generating a meagre and uneconomic 38,400 passenger journeys. However 1976 was a General Election Year (for seats in Tynwald) and the future of the steam railway became a political issue with various protagonists both 'for' and 'against' retention speaking out. The 'ayes' seemed to gain an ascendancy with newspaper reports that a Steering Committee of Tynwald had recommended that the Island's Government should subsidise steam trains to run on the Isle of Man Railway between Douglas and Port Erin, during the 1977 summer season.

The position would be reviewed in the autumn and a decision made as to whether the £40,000 subsidy should be continued, or the line compulsorily purchased as suggested by The Isle of Man Steam Railway Supporters Association Ltd.

The season was very successful, with passenger journeys at a healthy figure of 81,790. The idea of government ownership found favour and The Isle of Man Railway Co agreed to sell the line - and so took no part in its affairs after January 1978. Control passed to the Manx Electric Railway Board (acting on behalf of Tynwald). The M.E.R. Board's Chief Executive was Mr William Jackson, C.Eng. F.I.E.E. who was appointed in December 1977 to take charge of the Manx Electric and Snaefell Mountain Railways. Under Government ownership a substantial sum was spent on reconditioning rolling stock: rationalisation although unpalatable seemed inevitable and surplus land, buildings and other assets were sold, so releasing tied up capital.

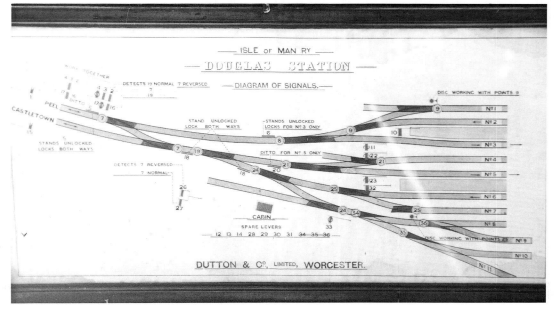

Isle of Man Railway. Douglas Station, Signal Box Diagram. c.1958.

This reproduction of the signalling diagram and station lay-out needs little comment, save to remark that of the levers shown as spare e.g. No.s 12, 13, 14, 28, 29, 30, 31, 34, 35 and 36, the last three are neatly 'scored through' having later been taken into use to operate ' shunts ' to Goods Roads No.s 10, 11, and 8, the Shunt to Road No.9 was ' normal '.

The late Ivor Vaughan: courtesy W.G.Rear.

(left) **Near Douglas. c.1958.** This view is of the Outer Home Signals which relate to the two independent Peel and Port Erin lines. Both 'Outer' and 'Inner' home signals are similarly numbered with No. 2. relating to the Peel line and No. 16 that for trains coming from the Port Erin direction. On the track plan these signals are designated as 'working together' and are operated by the same levers in the signal box. The Isle of Man Railway was of single line formation throughout with passing loops, all of which were within station limits, whilst traffic was worked on the Single Line Staff and Ticket System. Various distinctive shapes of staff were used, painted in different colours and imprinted with the names of the block stations. When tickets were used the last train through the section would hold the staff, the driver of any preceding train or trains - having seen the appropriate staff first - would be issued with a ticket of the same colour as the staff. The Train Staff for the section was used to unlock the relevant Ticket Box and a minimum ten-minute time interval was enforced between trains when Ticket-working was in operation. This was a completely manually operated system, but nevertheless one tried and tested by time and which handled traffic effectively and safely throughout the busiest periods of the Isle of Man Railway's existence.

Photo: The late Ivor Vaughan, courtesy W.G. Rear.

(right) **Douglas. c.1958.** The Douglas Outer Home Signals. This obverse side view highlights some interesting design features. Vandalism was unusual on the Isle of Man then, and it is regrettable that the spectacle lenses have been broken by stone throwing. Although the Isle of Man Railway stuck mainly - then - to the practice long abandoned 'over there', of 'Red' danger and 'White' all clear, when double spectacles were fitted the Red/Green convention applied. The wire cable attached to the length of chain carrying the pull upwards from the bottom pulley to the operating mechanism must have stretched to such a degree that the signalman was unable to work the semaphore arm correctly and the signal linesman has fastened a couple of old pulleys to the counter balance weights to increase their efficiency. The cantilever platform bracket displays another excellent example of wrought iron work, the square section main post having a graceful taper, functionalism combining with craftsmanship. A sturdy fixed ladder was provided for the lampman and the signal platform has a sensible guard rail. The ensemble is nicely complimented with neatly angled end-caps and finials, and the whole is secured by extended bracing wires against the onslaught of winter gales. The track appears in good fettle with the ballast free from weeds, whilst the cable run continuing in the grass beyond the signal post is en-route to the Distant Signal around the bend. On approaching this point, drivers of trains from Peel would sound one long blast on the whistle, in accordance with the Rules and Regulations, whilst drivers of trains from Port Erin and the south were enjoined to identify themselves by two long whistle blasts.

Photo: The late Ivor Vaughan: courtesy W.G. Rear.

Douglas. c.1958. Turning now to a 'rear' view of the Inner-Home Signals, we observe that the photographer has skilfully included - on the bend in the distance - a long range impression of co-acting Home Signals. The lateral lighting brings into focus the raised relief pattern on the plating of the water tanks, whilst the inner circular motif of the bracket supporting the signal platform is quite elaborate in style, the stability of the structure, perhaps because of its height, may have necessitated the provision of the iron tie-rods securing the platform edge to the wall. Reading from top to bottom, Signals No.2, 3 and 4 on the Peel line relate to Road No.3 and Road No.5 both Nos. 2 and 3 working in conjunction with the No.1 Distant Signal. To get the Peel Road required the use of Locking Bars Nos. 6, 5, whilst No.5 Road required Points No.7, with Locking Bars Nos.20, 18, 5 and, for the Goods Road, Points Nos. 7, 19 and 24 were needed with Locking Bars Nos. 18, 5 and signal No.4. As to the duo of signals on the other post, No.5 Road required No.15, the Port Erin Distant and Home Signal No.16 with Locking Bars Nos. 20 and 18, whilst for the Port Erin Goods Road it was Signals Nos. 17 and 15, Points Nos. 19 and 24, with Locking Bar No.18. Distant signal levers were coloured green, Stop signals red, Point levers black, Locking levers blue and Spares, white.

Photo: The late Ivor Vaughan: courtesy W.G. Rear.

Douglas Station c.1933. In the preceding decades, the British Empire had undergone the trauma of the Boer War(1899-1902), whilst the confidence of the Edwardians had been assailed by the loss of the 'unsinkable' White Star liner Titanic following her collision with an iceberg at about 11.40pm on Sunday night the 14th April 1912, whilst proceeding on her maiden voyage to New York at a speed of 22½ knots and, completing the trio of calamitious events that signalled the end of an epoch came the horror of the Great War (1914-1918). Nor had the Manx people yet recovered from the grevious blow of their own **'Black Saturday'** when the failure and closure of Dumbell's Bank on 3rd February 1900, brought financial ruin to many ordinary folk, as well as members of the business community. Yet, excepting for the addition of platform awnings the station, as seen from the signal box had altered little, in the ensuing years and the theme of continuity is maintained by the fussy perambulations of one of the Isle of Man Railway's inimitable 2-4-0T's marshalling stock near to the cross-over on the south side of the station, which gave access to the Goods Shed, Cattle Dock, Goods Platform and Low Level Sidings. Today's leaner, seasonal only Isle of Man Railway no longer requires this extensive layout, the platform awnings have gone, as have the tall signal gantries, colour light signals are in use and there is a large bus depot on the south side, but it is still recognisably Douglas Station and it is under the skilful care of Department of Transport, Chief Executive Robert Smith Esq., B.A. MCIT, and his staff being restored in a manner befitting this terminus of the doyen of narrow gauge railways.

The late H.C.Casserley collection:courtesy Richard Casserley.

Douglas Station.Friday 9th August 1963. With smokebox door open and crew deep in discussion, No.**5**.*Mona*, Beyer Peacock built 2-4-0T, (Work No.1417 of 1874) stands on the No.2 Platform line.Built with a small 120lb pressure boiler and 385 gallon tanks,her performance was enhanced by a chang to a larger, 160lb pressure boiler and 480 gallon water tanks. Mona, repainted under Lord Ailsa's regime was stored in the Carriage Shed at Douglas i 1986 and is now owned by The Isle of Man Railway Society. No.**8**.*Fenella* heads a Peel train in Platform No.3.The leading carriage F26 dates back to 189 and is the last of the F13-26 Series supplied by the Metropolitan Railway Carriage & Wagon Co., of Birmingham, who had acquired the firm of Messr Brown Marshalls & Co.,Ltd., designers of some early I.O.M.Rly carriages.Except for the inward waisted lower panels, the 35ft long x 7ft wide bodies wer very similar to the class F1-F6 which also ran on diamond-frame bogies.The internal layout was G/ 33/ 33/ 3.The Guard's compartment was full partitioned, but each of the two pairs of third class compartments were, when new, open internally above the seat backs.   *G.Biddle*

Douglas.Sunday. 19th August 1956. When a youthful Gregory K.Fox went to the I.O.M.with the 1st Romiley Scout Group he immediately fell in love with its trains and trams; appropriate therefore that he was snapped posing with the line's oldest engine, No.**1**. *Sutherland,* named in honour of the Chairman, the Duke of Sutherland. It arrived on the island from Liverpool on the morning of Thursday, 27th March 1873, together with a four-wheeled First Class carriage and a four-wheeled wagon fitted with wooden seats. A trial trip is thought to have been made on 1st May 1873, to show off the line to a group of officials (including the Duke) from the London & North Western and Lancashire & Yorkshire Railways, who broke their journey to Liverpool from Ireland, where they had been attending the opening of the Dundalk & Greenore Railway on 30th April 1873. The group,which included the B.O.T Inspector Col.Rich landed at Peel and were taken to Douglas by road to sample the embyro Isle of Man Railway.   *The late Cyril Fox.*

Douglas. 16th July 1962. No.11 *Maitland* in brown (umber) livery, stands on the engine service road, framed by signals No.s.11 and 22, looking with their spiky finials, dumpy posts and hefty ladders rather like model railway signals. No.11, named after an official of the company, displays a Beyer Peacock works plate on the cab side-sheet, and was one of two engines to arrive in 1905. Slightly larger than their pre-decessors, although of the same basic design, No.s.10,11,12 and 13 had 3 ft 3 ins diameter boilers, 480 gallon side-tanks, a three inch extension of the driving wheelbase and a five inch overall increase in height at the cab roof. Later alterations saw the open bell-mouthed dome and Salter spring-balance safety valves replaced by the more practical 'Pop' type valve.   *Norman Jones.*

Douglas.16th July 1962. The platforms could each hold two trains of normal length, the handsome awnings which continue from the glazed circulating area were added in 1905 when the facilities were vastly improved. No attempt was made to hide the functional nature of the structure with sham Doric or Ionian columns; the roof rests on heavy Channel Girders, set vertically in massive concrete footings, the cladding and glazing pitches covering a practical framework of angled cross girders and triangular trusses. No.8 *Fenella* is seen shunting the stock for a Port Erin train, usually Down trains would leave from the outer platform faces, whilst the inner were reserved for arrivals from the Up direction.   *Norman Jones.*

Douglas Station. Post World War II. The clock in the tower above the entrance on the corner of Peel Road reads 4 p.m. as No.6. *Peveril* arouses the echoes beneath the splendid platform awnings. Both No.6. and No.8. *Fenella* bore names immortalised by the writings of Sir Walter Scott. Peveril was fitted with a 'closed dome' and 'pop' safety valves in 1934, and further improved by the fitting of a 3ft 3ins diameter boiler, 480 gallon Water Tanks and a Wakefield mechanical lubricator. The leading coach F24 is one of the series numbered F12-F26 supplied by the Metropolitan Carriage & Wagon Co., thought to date from about 1895 the compartment configuration was G/3/1/1/3 3.

W.G.Rear: Ivor Vaughan collection.

Douglas. 16th July 1962. No.**10**. *G.H.Wood*, (Works No.4662 of 1905) blows off energetically against a fine display of vintage I.O.M.Rly vehicles. The second carriage behind No.10 is F22, one of the Metropolitan Carriage & Wagon Co., F13-26 batch. To the left of the engine is Van G8, now a covered van loading 6 ton on a tare weight of 3 tons, originally built by the M.C.&.W.Co.as a dual purpose, e.g. 'Covered Goods Van/Third Class Carriage' to drawings of 22nd November 1872. Six were on hand for the opening of the line; they had double-opening central doors, beneath which were double footsteps and longtitudinal drop-down seats. They were 14ft 6ins long x 6ft 6ins wide and 8ft 11 ins high; the 2ft 3ins diameter wheels were set on a wheelbase of 8ft 10ins. The batch was completely rebuilt for goods only work and a circular 'port-hole', with a wooden drop-down flap in the side-panels was a feature of all the Class excepting G3, alterations were also made to the braking system.   *Norman Jones.*

Douglas Station. c.1928. Adding to the indubitable character of the Isle of Man locomotives was the rather dashing, sloping smoke box front, which combined with the inclined cylinders, open topped dome and Salter spring balance safety valves, gave them a slightly raffish, devil may care look, so it was not surprising perhaps that in the formative years a re-railing jack carried on the right hand side tank should be an indispensable part of their equipment. A wooden tool box was mounted the opposite side. Built in this mode was No.**7** *Tynwald* (Beyer, Peacock Works No.2038 of 1880), one of the series of 'small boilered' engines that ended with the delivery of No.**9** Douglas in 1896. However, during the 'salad days' of the Isle of Man Railway, improvements and modifications were made and, in 1925, Tynwald was fitted with a 'Pop' valve in the dome, the elegant 'Salter' valves being removed and a further 'Pop' valve mounted centrally on the boiler barrel between the chimney and dome, both fittings obligingly displaying their presence by emitting feathers of steam for the photographers. No.**7** Tynwald was dismantled in 1945 and the chassis, stored at Port Erin was latterly acquired by the Isle of Man Railway Society.

H.Townley:courtesy J.M.Bentley.

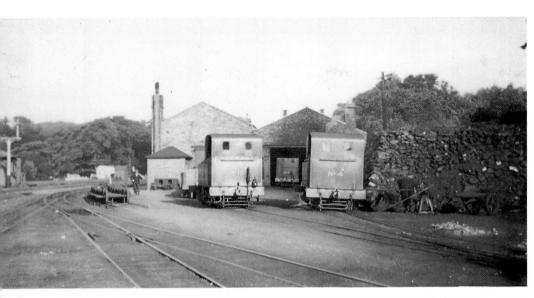

Douglas Station. c.1937. The appearance of the I.O.M.Rly's workshops and loco-shed at Douglas changed little over the years. An unidentified locomotive lurks just inside the entrance to the shed, whilst No.4. *Loch*, named after a former Lieutenant Governor of the island is also on parade. An unchanging feature is the serried rank of redundant wheels and axles, whilst a lot of patience has gone into the stacking of the reserve coal supplies.
P.H.Abell collection.

Douglas. 16th July 1962. Featuring Carriage No.F7. c.1875 Messrs Brown Marshalls & Co. submitted to the I.O.M.Rly drawings for coaches with bodies 35ft long, 7ft 0ins wide and 9ft 4ins high from rail to roof centre, intended as replacements for the original and out-dated four-wheelers. Delivery was made over a period of time the the first of the series F1-F6 were running c.1880. A further batch F7-F12 was ordered and delivered in 1881, the makers' plate was fixed to the bottom skirting on each side. On 1st January 1875 the Midland Railway abolished second -class and re-labelled all its former second class compartments as third. The I.O.M.Rly followed suit in July 1878 so that F7 went into service with compartments allocated G/3/1/1/3/3. The 4ft 6ins wheelbase diamond-frame bogies were 25ft 10ins apart, the wheels were spoked, the slab-sided lower panels masked the framing and sole-bars and the Guard's compartment had three rear-end observation windows.
Photo:the late H.C.Casserley: courtesy Richard Casserley.

Douglas. 20th April 1950. A composite photo, showing the end of F7, Brake/compo F40 and the leading end of F37, a former Manx Northern vehicle. Supplied in 1908/9 by the M.C.&.W.Co. the small batch including F40 were fitted, as new with Stones Duplex Electric Lighting, the accumulators were housed in a locker fixed to the floor of the luggage section. The 'Stone' system of electric carriage lighting although it became the most favoured was not the first, Matthew Holmes experimented with electric lighting on the North British Railway about 1880, as did William Stroudley on the London, Brighton & South Coast Railway, and Mr.F.W.Webb of the 'Nor-West' had a train electrically lit by a steam donkey engine driving a dynamo, mounted on the former tender of an old Ramsbottom express engine. Mr J.Stone patented his single battery system in 1894 and made the final break-through in 1896 with the double-battery system, the hall-mark of the 'Stone 'system being the lightweight under-floor dynamo driven from one of the revolving carriage axles.
The late H.C.Casserley:courtesy Richard Casserley.

Douglas.20th April.1950. Carriage F20 of the C13-26 series shared with F19 the distinction of being the first of its kind supplied to the I.O.M..Rly. The body housed three separate Third Class compartments, plus a Guard's and Luggage compartment with double-doors. Station Master Crellin said that some of the items carried might be : Empty wooden coffins 1/6d (7.1/2p), ditto, accompanied by Adult, 10/0d. (50p), whilst a piano cost 2/6d (25p), and a wheelbarrow 4d (.16p), one wonders if the piano arrived on the wheelbarrow? Until the 1920's when moves were made towards vacuum braking on the I.O.M.Rly, brakesmen posted in strategic carriages worked with the guard in stopping trains by means of handbrakes. The method of working was detailed in the rule book which specified places at which brakes were applied. Guards and Brakesmen were were instructed not to converse with passengers.

Photo: The late H.C.Casserley: Courtesy Richard Casserley.

Douglas.20th April 1950. In 1905 the M.C.&.W.Co. began delivering some fine saloon carriages in the F29-32 and F35-36 series. They had a modern appearance, the body sides ending above the solebars which were exposed, together with the Truss-rods, Queen-posts and other under-floor fittings. The bodies measured 36ft 11ins long x 7ft 0ins wide, height 10ft 3ins from rail level to roof centre line. A central gangway ran through each saloon compartment and access was by end doors into a vestibule with glazed ends. The Third class saloon had seven glazed windows, whereas F36 a 1st/3rd compo. had eight- the diamond frame, 4ft 6ins wheelbase bogies ran on 2ft 3ins diameter spoked wheels.

Photo: The late H C.Cassserley: Courtesy Richard Casserley.

Douglas.20th April.1950. The Manx Northern Rly. ordered two very similar coaches from Messrs.Hurst Nelson & Co.Ltd., of Glasgow in 1899. The only two such vehicles that the M.N.Rly owned, they were taken into I.O.M.Rly stock when it absorbed the M.N.Rly in 1904 to become No.s F37-38. They were steel framed coaches and the M.N.Rly scored over the senior company by being the first to have coaches fitted from new with Stones electric lighting system. The bodies were 35ft 6ins long and 7ft 0.3/4ins wide, but whereas F37 (illustrated) had the compartment layout of G/3/1/1/3/3 , in the case of F38 a Third class compartment replaced the Guard's. F37 is seen to be vacuum fitted, whereas F38 was only 'piped through', the interiors were nicely upholstered in accordance with the standards of the time.

Photo: The late H.C.Casserley: Courtesy Richard Casserley.

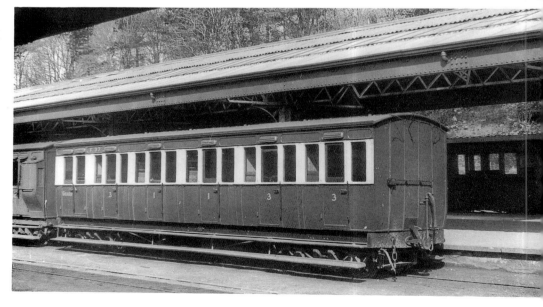

Port Soderick. May 1979. Were it not for the road sign stating the available clearance to be 11ft 0ins or 3.35 metres, this photograph might have been taken any time within the last 100 years. The rail journey from Douglas to Port Soderick is always exhilarating, with the sturdy Beyer Peacock engines slogging their way through curves, and cuttings, surmounting the long 1 in 85 gradient. Just before entering the wooded confines of the station the line curves left, and the metals are carried across the narrow road which leads down to Port Soderick bay by this attractive bridge.
D. Ibbotson.

Port Soderick. c.1967. No.8 *Fenella* has called with a Douglas - Castletown train during the 'Ailsa' period, when it seemed that there was to be a memorable resurgence of the entire Isle of Man Railway network, and possibly a return to happier days for this once much favoured tourist haunt. Indeed it was so popular as the century neared its turn - very much as a result of the excursion trains promoted by the I.O.M.Rly, that in 1896 a run-round loop was installed, and the station rebuilt, with the present slab-edged platform and attractive station buildings. *Photo: P.H.Abell collection.*

Santon. Summertime. c.1960. No.8. *Fenella* is approaching Santon, the next station south from Port Soderick with a mixed train from Douglas, the wagon and three assorted vans' hung on 'in the rear probably for Castletown. Almost midway between Port Soderick and Santon the site of the abandoned Ballacostain Halt was marked by a small, grassy mound on the north side of the tracks, close to a stone overbridge. The halt, built about 1910 was used mainly by members of the Officers Training Chore from the King William's College, and later Territorial forces, all of whom travelled to practice on the nearby Pistol Castle Rifle Range. As the line descends towards the area of low lying land stretching from Derbyhaven to Port St.Mary, on a clear day there are views across to St.Michael's Isle, Dreswick and Langness Points and the Herring Tower, now on the 'protected buildings register' and built by Thomas Brine about 1818 after the style of the classic 'round towers' in Peel.
W.G.Rear.

Ballasalla.Sept 1967. During the shortage of available locomotives following an unfortunate collission at Union Mills , (referred to elsewhere),the former Manx Northern Railway's 0-6-0T locomotive No.*4 Caledonia*(No.15. in the I.O.M.Rly's stocklist) was pressed into service. Ballasalla was a 'crossing place' and the two train crews may well be discussing the steaming capabilities of the relief engine. From the ferocity and height of the chimney emissions one would assume that the blower is 'full on' probably to counter the loss of front end integrity, as surely an airtight seal could not be achieved with such a badly dented smoke-box door. *P.H.Abell..*

Castletown.c.1930. An evocative glimpse of the island's former capital between the wars,with No.10 *G.H.Wood* at the head of a train bound for Port Erin. It was certainly a less casual age,with,in evidence,'donkey's breakfast' straw hats and voluminous lightweight coats summer wear for the womenfolk.Umbrell were often carried'at the ready', unfurled for use equally against the sun as the rain - the cult of the sun-worshipper was not yet come. No shortage of passenge either,with every carriage door open,the throng scrambling for window seats and a uniformed porter swept along in the crush.I would propose that it was a hot,ha day with thunderstorms threatening,as several of the gents carry their raincoats. No.10 G.H.Wood was the first engine to be modified with a closed dome a 'pop'valves and with a Tractive Effort of 6,580 lbs was appreciably more powerful than No.s.l to 9,who could each only produce 4,930 lbs T.E.

H.C.Casserley collection:courtesy Richard Casserle

Castletown.c.1960. The largest and most powerful of the I.O.M.Rly's engines, and the last to be built for the Co.was No.**16** *Mannin*.(Works No.6296 of 1926), seen en-route to Port S.Mary and Port Erin. Mannin had a new style of cab, larger and square cornered,cylinders were o/s 12ins diameter by 18ins stroke, the 3ft 6ins boiler was pressed at 180 lbs p.s.i and the T.E.was 8,810 lbs.

The leading coach, F54 in the F50-75 Series was made up from the bodies of old four-wheeled carriages that were, at one time close-coupled in pairs and later with running gear removed, mounted in pairs onto new bogie under-frames. These were supplied by the M.C.&.W.Co., and this particular conversion was carried out in 1923. Over the years the (piped only) vehicles could be electrically lit, but only by connecting them to an adjoining carriage equipped with the 'Stone' system. The brake compartment was retained exactly as when the body ran as a four-wheeler. *W.G.Rear.*

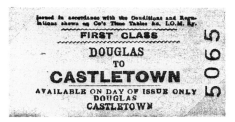

Castletown.May 1979. This fine example of a slotted post signal could be viewed without entering onto railway property standing,as it did. beside the Castletown - Port Erin road.It could very well have attained its century when the photograph was taken and is very similar to one which I examined at Santon in 1962.It is gratifying that this survivor had not attracted vandals and still possesses intact its lamp,mounted on a tall vertical spindle which,when rotated turned the light and changed the colour aspect in conjunction with the raising or lowering of the semaphore arm.The earliest signals are thought to have been supplied by A.Linley & Co.later The Linley Engineering Co.,Ltd., of Birmingham,who also supplied the operating windlasses which were often installed near the centre of a station platform. *D.Ibbotson.*

Castletown.Sunday.11th August 1963. Looking north towards Douglas.Castletown was the seat of government until supplanted by Douglas in 1869.Traffic-wise it was probably the next most important station to Douglas on the island and acquired the handsome station buildings,a fine slate roofed goods shed but, oddly not a platform in improvements made about 1900.   The Castletown Brewery used rail transport,as did the local gas works,more traffic came from fishing boats unloading in the harbour and local industries made their contribution.Trains were usually mixed and 'fly' shunting,long banned from Britain's main line railways was carried out regularly and safely by I.O.M.Rly employees.Two sidings were reached via a facing point at the eastern end of the Down loop,one line running into the Goods Shed and the other continuing behind the station buildings.
Gordon Biddle

Colby.c.1960. No.**11** *Maitland* seen on the 10.a.m.Douglas-Port Erin train and built in 1905 was the second of the batch of 2-4-0T's to be fitted with the 3ft 3ins boiler and 480 gallon water tanks. In 1981 she would be rebuilt with a much larger 3ft 7ins boiler, new side tanks and a large, square, 'Mannin' style cab.Journeying from Castletown No.11 has passed the site of the disused Ballabeg Halt climbing easily towards Colby.Although in the formative years the long stretch of single line between Port Erin and Castletown caused appreciable delays, it was not until 1907 that the Colby passing loop was installed;if necessary trains could then be crossed at every station between Douglas and Port Erin. No.**11** was photographed from a train on the 'opposing' working; the 'actual'time for the 12¾. mile run Douglas-Colby where the Down train was booked to 'Pass-Slow for Loop and Staff' was 53 minutes.

Courtesy G.Fox Collection.

Port.St.Mary.Sunday 11th August 1963. Although the earliest I.O.M.Rly signals were of the slotted-post type, this Up Home signal, a lower quadrant design is of a later pattern, where the lens centre is parallel with the centre-line of the arm. Both Messrs Linley and Stevens, respected names in the field supplied the railway with signalling equipment. The post is incomplete, lacking either cap or finial, possibly destroyed when the lens was broken. When in full working order the aspects would have been Red for Danger and White for All Clear. The fixed ladder, platform and guardrail are not very strong and the rigidity of the ladder has been improved by the addition of a bracing bar tying its base to the signal post. *Gordon Biddle.*

Port.St.Mary.11th August 1963. Folk lore relates that 'The Harbour of Mary' was named after the Virgin Mary by Celtic missionaries who landed here and built a small Keill, or chapel; the site lies beneath the Town Hall buildings, the landing is commemorated by Chapel Beach. It is a favourite resort for yachtsmen and was so popular in the 1890's that the I.O.M.Rly's 1898 rebuilding programme included these handsome station buildings, with an impresssive platform, Goods Shed, Goods Platform and Cattle Dock, not forgetting a handsome hotel. The stature of the buildings surpasses those of Castletown and are second in size only to those at Douglas. The buildings abound in architectural mores of the time, from the circular columns rising from square pedestals with a cushioned cap to effect the transition in shape, decorated barge boards, a 'corbelled' upper window, leaded roofs, decorated quoins to overhanging eaves, in fact the whole gamut of 'Municipal' style architecture at its eclectic best. *Gordon Biddle.*

Port.St.Mary Station.May 1979. The clock in the booking-office window recorded 10.55am when the photographer took this picture which, excepting for the currently dated 'Steam Railway' time-table might have been taken at any time during the present century.The architectural complexities of the rather fine building are further evident from this camera angle, whilst to the right is observed the 'running on' or name-board and the Goods Shed, built in a style complementary to the other hereditaments, the Cattle Dock was located opposite to the Goods Platform.
                                    D.Ibbotson.

Port St.Mary Station.May 1979. The I.O.M.Rly's rebuilding programme certainly produced a very commanding structure as this frontal aspect confirms.But this genteel resort was steadily growing in popularity.The Old Pier,615 feet in length was opened in 1845,cost £8,200 to build,and provided a good anchorage for small craft.The(then)Duke of Edinburgh opened the 930 foot long Alfred Pier in 1882;this cost £39,000 to build and included a deep-water berth. The I.O.M.Rly Co.,therefore had an incentive to provide a station of suitable munificence for the upper and middle-class visitors who found the select surroundings of Port St.Mary so much to their liking.   *D.Ibbotson.*

Nr.Port St.Mary.May 1979. Although the design of the level crossing gates, including the diagonal bracing,is identical the structure of the accompanying house at a location on the Isle of Man Railway's Castletown-Port Erin line differs to that illustrated later, whereas the Crossing Keeper's cottage at Ballacrye on the former Manx Northern line to Ramsey is seen to be much more homely in its appearance, indeed the additional cowl perched on the castellated chimney pot of the I.O.M.Rly's building gives it a rather raffish, dissolute air. *D.Ibbotson.*

Port Erin.c.1960. The spacious platform was added during a re-building programme that was finished in time for the Whitsundtide holiday of 1904, and as this south-western port and watering place became even more popular the platform was lengthened again in 1911. Presently, the resort is experiencing a 'mini-boom' with the Port Erin Hotels' chain reporting a record figure of 10,553 guests during 1990. The splendid bay is dominated by the bold outline of Bradda Head, crowned by Milner's Tower, erected by public subsccription in memory of William Milner a local benefactor who was untiring in his efforts to improve the lot of all Manx fishermen. *C.L.Caddy.*

Port Erin. July 1962. Close to the standing figure in the preceding photograph may be seen the facing connection leading to the Water-tank and Loco-shed, before the open doors of which poses No. **16** *Mannin*, Works No. 6296 of 1926, the largest and most powerful of the I.O.M. Rly's stud of Beyer Peacock built 2-4-0T's and, at that time, the only member to have the large, square cornered cab which afforded the locomotive crew a greater measure of weather protection than did the wrap-over version on the older engines.

D. Ibbotson.

Port Erin. Monday. 12th August 1963. An immaculate No. **10**. *G.H. Wood* is overshadowed by the Water-tank high on a massive masonry base; the control gear at the top of the inspection ladder is worthy of note, as is the enormous valve, and hand wheel, projecting at the lower, left hand corner. Assorted fire-irons are balanced behind the re-railing jack carried on No. 10's right-hand tank top and the narrow bunker inside the cab is filled to its full 14 cwt capacity. This is a beautifully crisp photograph and should be of particular interest to modellers, details of the pony-truck, sand-pipes and brake-rigging stand out clearly and it is even possible to count the number of rivets on the tank sides.

G. Biddle.

Port Erin. Wednesday. 18th September 1963. The author and his colleague had just alighted from the x. County Donegal railcars, after a spirited trip from Douglas, well patronised, we were pleased to note by local people, travelling between intermediate stations. Furthermore, a substantial amount of parcels traffic was conveyed in the 'G' type van which, sandwiched between the two rail cars made its presence felt every time we passed over a 'fished' joint. The four-coupled power-bogies of these articulated railcars were built by Walker Bros. of Wigan and were the last to be built for the County Donegal Joint Committee. Each was powered by a 6LW Gardner Oil engine. The makers delivered the cab-units complete, but the carriage portion was built at Dundalk in the former Great Northern Railway Works. The drive was transmitted through a Meadows four-speed gear box and orthodox propellor shaft to the rear axle.
Photo: The late Herbert Woodward.

Port Erin. 12th August 1963. What a handsome building this is. A fine set of finials adorn the gables of the transverse buildings and different styles of embellishment were employed. Left, beneath the corbels supporting the mock Jacobean framing the cornice consists of a line of half-round plinth-stretcher bricks, whilst the right-hand side gable has a geometrical pattern in relief. The windows in the further gable end follow the convention sometimes called 'Mill-engine Gothic' reminiscent of the stately 'chapels' that housed the steam engines of Lancashire's Mills. Now, almost thirty years since the photograph was taken and ninety years since Messrs. McArd & Moore laid the last red Ruabon brick, the station is magnificently restored to ' as new ' condition, with Mr Bob Weston, the Station Master the proud holder, on behalf of the Isle of Man Railway, of an Ian Allan Heritage Award Commendation, presented by British Rail Chairman, Sir Bob Reid. *G.Biddle.*

Kirk Braddan Halt.c.1968. The simplicity of the halt, a wide stretch of land beside the tracks and a wooden Booking Hut belied it's one-time importance. It was the next stopping place (after the Quarter Bridge Halt was closed), on the Douglas-Peel line and was used by worshippers attending the open-air religous services, held in the natural ampitheatre behind Kirk Braddan New Church, consecrated in 1876. The site was, however of some antiquity, a Synod was held here in 1229 and Runic Crosses found nearby have Norse connotations. Before and between the two World Wars congregations of around 20,000 were usual during the seasons. These figures were not attained post World War II, but a special Sunday service of trains was well patronised. The first train usually loaded to ten coaches and other workings might follow 'as required'. After unloading the E.C.S. was taken to Union Mills, so that the engine might 'run-round', the departure time depending on the length of the service. No.**5.**_Mona_ waits for the returning worshippers, as do the booking-staff, in attendance to deal with visitors who had walked up from Douglas but wished to ride back. The picture was taken from the bridge which carries the A1 Douglas-Peel highway across the line, originally narrow and stone built the bridge was rebuilt in more modern form, using steel spans in October 1912. *C.L.Caddy.*

Crosby.c.1967. The driver and Station Master confer as ex C.D.Railcars No.s.**19 & 20.** wait for the level crossing gates to be opened for the continuance of their journey from Peel, the next level crossing they will negotiate is at Closemoar. In the long grass to the right of the gates is the Linley Signal Winch which worked the Down Home Signal. Behind the photographer was a small overbridge across the River Greeba, near which was a 'limit of shunt' post. Rule No.297 described this as a white post placed at the end of a loop line, or through sidings entering a main line at a station. Engines were not to pass unless given permission by the person in charge of the station. During the hours of darkness a white light was to be displayed on the post. Near to Crosby was Greeba Castle, the home of Sir Hall Caine, the famous Manx novelist, also the ruins of St.Trinians Church, dedicated to a 4th century Celtic Bishop.   *C.L.Caddy.*

Crosby.c.1967. Another picture taken during the locomotive shortage when 0-6-0T, the former M.N.Rly _Caledonia_, appeared at the head of a three coach Douglas-Peel train, she looks, apart from the dented smoke-box door, quite smart and has obviously received some cosmetic attention. The smoke-box wings give her an antiquated as well as a Scottish air, the latter fitting her ancestry. Hidden in the long grass is the lower set of rails that formed a facing (from the St.John's end) connection with the loop-nearby lay the Cattle Dock and Goods Shed. Caledonia must have only just entered station limits, as the level crossing gates across the road that led southwards to Braaid, near where are the remains of some Celtic and Nordic houses classified as Ancient Monuments, have not yet been closed.   *C.L.Caddy.*

Union Mills.c.1937. A train from Douglas, bound for St John's and Peel leaves Union Mills in the palmy days of the Isle of Man Railway. The protruding 'ducket' of the guard's van is a prominent feature of this shot taken from a rear compartment, and the guard is looking forward to confirm, as instructed by the rules, that an 'orderly departure' is being made, this delightfully located station is situated on a reverse curve, the station buildings are on the right; there was a concrete platform on the Down side only and not far from the station was the site of an old race-course.
P.H.Abell Collection.

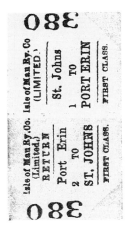

Carriage Shed St.John's.Saturday 28th July.1962. The long, corrugated-iron carriage shed which was built in 1905 and lay parallel to the main line was destroyed by fire on a December night seven decades later. The line-up of former Manx Northern Railway six-wheeled coaches depicted here had seen very little use for about twenty years. They were delivered to the M.N.Rly in 1879, although some of the axle-boxes were dated 1877. Of the total of fifteen of this type of coach with Cleminson trucks, supplied by the Swansea Wagon Co.Ltd., it would seem that two were at some time replaced by two Hurst Nelson bogie carriages, the body of one coach was taken to Douglas and used as a Mess Hut near the loco-sheds and the other was believed to have been at Ramsey, but had been scrapped by the 1960's. The 'Cleminson' coaches were placed in a series N40-N51, in the I.O.M.Rly's stock list, this letter being the next available after the prefix 'M' which was applied to the class of open four-wheeled goods wagons.
J.H.Price.MCIT.

St. John's. ex Manx Northern Signals. 12th August 1963. This fine example of a 'slotted post' signal was the No.8 Up Starting signal which, via Points Lever No.4. gave access to the Douglas line. The lamp rotated in conjunction with the movement of the semaphore arm to show either a red aspect for 'danger' or a white one for 'all clear'. The signal-box contained a ten lever frame, with tappet locking and was supplied by Messrs Stevens & Sons, whilst a nine lever frame from the same suppliers was located on the Foxdale Branch platform; it was not enclosed in a cabin, but a removeable iron strap could be padlocked across the quadrant plate to prevent tampering. The line immediately in front of the signal box - and the corrugated iron carriage shed- was the Ramsey line, the other two being, respectively, the Peel line and the loop line. When the shed was destroyed on Wednesday 10th December 1975 the damage was extensive, and only charred remnants and twisted chassis remained of a number of valuable carriages and the two coaches, destined for preservation, that were stored inside.   *G. Biddle.*

St. John's. Wednesday. 18th July. 1962. The salient features at the east end of the junction : the slotted post Starting signal is lowered, and the guard has given permission for the train to start. In the foreground we note a handsome fluted 'oil lamp' type post, neatly converted for electric lighting. The nearest coach F35 is one of the conversions of the early four-wheelers, done piecemeal fashion between 1910 and 1926, the bogie underframes being supplied by the Metropolitan Railway, Carriage & Wagon Co. A nine inch gap was left between the inner ends of the bodies to prevent condensation forming, but these had mostly been covered over by the time the photograph was taken, although the join is quite distinct: the stock looked very smart in the bright red and cream livery of that period.   *Norman Jones.*

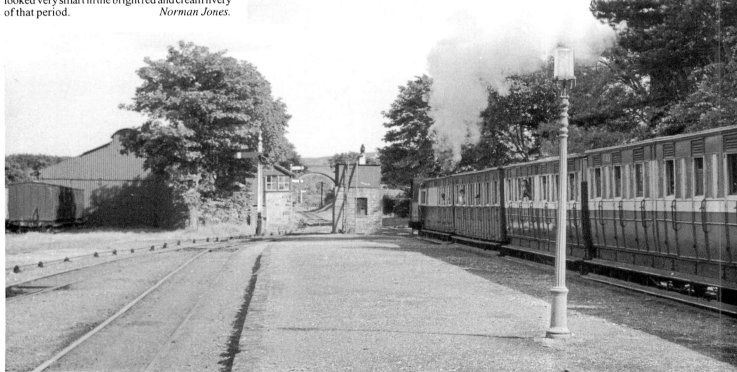

John's.c.1968. A study of the activity at the I.O.M.Rly's Clapham Junction during the Marquess of Ailsa's epoch, when there were hopes that the ovision of specialised freight wagons might win back some of the traffic lost, over the years, to road haulage. Quite a 'body' of passengers are about join a train standing on the Ramsey line and the 'Target Board' on the end coach should be noted; at this time some amendments were being made to e Company's Rules and Regulations, that had withstood the passage of time and remained unchanged for decades, so as to bring operating practices more line with those 'over there'. A 'mixed' train, typical of the new approach is seen in charge of No.11. *Maitland* (running with a laterally cracked rear buffer am), the freight component being an example of the 'new' tank wagons, which had been fabricated and mounted on redundant coach bogies.

C.L.Caddy.

John's. Monday. 16th July. 1962. No.10. *G.H.Wood* approaches the level crossing at the west end of the station with a train from Peel, the leading coach F19 being rake/composite. In the far distance, behind the last vehicle is the (lowered) semaphore arm of the Peel line signal, which was worked from St.Johns. The train rossing a small overbridge and on the right is the site of the Manx Northern's first station of 1879, alterations to the layout were necessary when through running tween the two companies over the Ramsey and St.John's-Douglas lines commenced in 1881. Further alterations took place when the Foxdale Railway opened 1896 and but for the arrival of these two concerns doubtless St.John's would never have been anything more exciting than a quiet country station.

Norman Jones.

St.John's.16th July.1962.If rail vehicles have a soul - and who am I to deny that - then the ex.Country Donegal railcars must have been reminded of their nati▮ Stranorlar, when they called at St.Johns.in that both places were important junctions on a busy system, enjoying periods of seeming somnolence, replaced by hect▮ activity and purposeful officials wher. trains arrived, almost simultaneously, from all points of the compass. St.John's is the third station (bearing the name) to ha▮ been situated hereabouts, eacl, being a further development or enlargement of that built in 1874. On the platform, watching No.10.G.H.Wood bring a train ov▮ the level crossing and slow for a stop in the station, is Mr.Jack Cretney, of the Isle of Man's Tourist Board, to the right of the Tynwald Day flagpole film cameram▮ the late Herbert Woodward concentrates on 'panning' the progress of the Douglas bound train.   *Norman Jone▮*

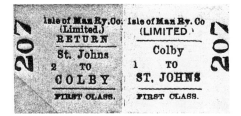

St.John's.16th July.1962.No.10 looked extremely smart,in umber livery,with bright red buffer beams,black smoke-box, highly polished name and works plates,and the dome dazzling with the almost silvery sheen only attained by a liberal and loving application of 'elbow-grease' and the appropriate unguent. The vintage locomotive is enhanced by an equally vintage F19 carriage which,with its running mate F20 were the first composites with inward waisted side panels that the I.O.M.Rly owned.They were built by the Metropolitan Railway,Carriage & Wagon Co,who had acquired the firm of Brown Marshall's who built the early four-wheelers.   *Norman Jones.*

St.John's.20th September.1962.The 'M' class wagon, a typical narrow gauge vehicle destined for Peel, is being manually propelled along the platform loop for attachment to the train, headed by No.10.G.H.Wood, halted over the level crossing. Other interesting items are the display adverts, notably the '*DAY EXCURSIONS TO DUBLIN AND BELFAST*' of the Isle of Man Steam Packet Co. The green and cream painted wooden station building was delightful of its type and the lady about to enter the Booking Hall would savour a delightful conglomerate of polish, old books and the scents of the Manx countryside. A guard rail deterred passengers, or station staff, unwittingly stepping into the path of a train.
Norman Jones.

t.John's.20th September.1962.No.10 *G.H.Wood* has now halted between the gates of the level crossing and Stationmaster George Crellin eases the wagon up against the rear coach,to which it will be secured by the centre-buffer coupling and side chains.The load of agricultural machinery,includes spares in an upside-own Heinz 57 Varieties carton.The 6 ton capacity wagon, tare weight approx.3 tons,is one of the four wheeled M1-M78 series,of a design which underwent only inor detail variations from the earliest days until the M.C.&.W.Co.supplied the last batch about 1925.The last lot were slightly larger bodied than their predecessors ing 14ft 6ins long and 6ft 6ins wide on a 8ft 0ins wheelbase,they ran on 2ft 3½ ins diameter Mansell wheels. Richard Mansell of the South Eastern Railway patented s wooden railway carriage wheels in 1848 and fitted them to the famous six-wheeled Chariot-ended Royal Saloon he built for that company.The basis of a Mansell heel was the centre of hardwood segments constrained by,at first an iron tyre,later steel,they were extensively used especially on coaching stock, by many railway mpanies.
Norman Jones.

St.John's.20th September.1962. The very popular St.John's Stationmaster, the late, Mr.George Crellin, collects the official mail (in the canvas bag)from Mr.Jack Watterson of Port Erin, as the railcars halt at the station on a Peel-Douglas working.Mr Crellin also holds the distinctive Peel-St.John's Section Train Staff and its appearance may be contrasted with that for the forward section shown in the next picture. The name of St.John's is closely linked with that of the nearby Tynwald Hill where annually on (Old) Midsummers Day the laws for the forthcoming year are promulgated, according to ancient custom, before what was, traditionally a huge gathering, comprising members of the Manx Legislative Council and the House of Keys, together with a Member of, or Representative of the Royal Family and elements of the general public,local business leaders and the like. Another important monument in the vicinity is the **MANX NATIONAL WAR MEMORIAL,** a fine and dignified Celtic Cross hewn from Scotch granite.

St.John's. 20th September.1962. When the rules are followed meticulously the Single Line Staff (or Staff and Ticket) system for working two-way traffic over a single line of railway is dependable. More sophisticated systems could fail due to human error, as witness the Abermule disaster on the Cambrian Railways in 1921; indeed Board of Trade Inspectors regarded a single line of railway as being incomplete. Passing loops on the I.O.M.Rly were within station limits, so each station was a Staff Exchange Point. The Driver and Station Master were jointly responsible for the proper control of the Staff, which was to be verified and approved by the Guard, before he permitted the train to start. It was the duty of the Stationmaster, or 'person in charge of the station ' to advise the 'person in charge'at the station in the rear that the train which they had despatched, had arrived. Until this confirmation was received no further train must be allowed to enter the section. In the case of double-headed trains the driver of the Pilot-engine was to hold the Staff, whereas elsewhere the driver of the Train-engine was the person so designated. Stationmaster the late George Crellin is displaying the Crosby-St.John's Staff.   *Norman Jones.*

.John's.Thursday.20th September 1962.No.10.*G.H.Wood*, it's tall, graceful 'Gorton' chimney replaced by one of more utilitarian outline, draws slowly over e level-crossing at the western end of the station, the driver looking back to ensure that the rear of his train is clear of the trailing connection with the south-side op, along which one wagon is being man-handled to join his train. Ahead the Peel and Ramsey lines diverge, to go their separate ways and it was customary for ins which left together to indulge in a spot of 'racing' although the Peel line train usually came out the winner, soon having the gradients in its favour. **AS TO ACING.** The very first Manx motor cycle Tourist Trophy races were held on Tuesday 28th May 1907, over a triangular course which started - and ended - at John's; the route was via Ballacraine, Kirkmichael and Peel. 25 riders started in the event which was really as much in the nature of a 'reliability' trial as anything se, 10 finished the course and the speed of the fastest lap over the 15 miles 1,430 yard circuit was 42.91 m.p.h. There were two classes, one for single, the other lti-cylindered machines; weight, and engine capacity, were unlimited but there was a restriction on the amount of fuel consumed. Records show that the weather as as fickle then, as now and it is interesting to note that **pedalling gear** was banned in 1909, and restrictions on fuel consumption dropped. *Norman Jones.*

St.John's.Friday.21st September.1962. The transport monopoly enjoyed by the island's railways and tramways was threatened in the late 1920's when powers were granted to the mainland based coach proprietors, Cumberland Motor Services Ltd., to operate on a few specific routes out of Douglas; in 1927 this company ran Manxland Bus Services, a company registered in the island. The Isle of Man Railway Co. countered by taking up shares in the Manx based motor bus operators, Manx Motors Ltd. Rivalry was fierce but in a very similar manner to that in which the Steam Packet Co. had overwhelmed interlopers, the competing organisations were acquired by the Isle of Man Railway Co. and Isle of Man Road Services was formed on Monday, 30th June.1930. Afterwards the road and rail services worked in conjunction, with a rationalisation of publicity and advertising, time-tables etc. a *ROAD SERVICES TIME-TABLE* was displayed beside the booking-office window at St. John's, and amongst other services publicised were those radiating to Ramsey, Kirkmichael, Glen Wyllin, Peel, Foxdale and Castletown. *Norman Jones.*

St.John's.Monday.12th August.1963. An age gap of fifty years separates No.16.*Mannin*, in charge of a Peel train from No.5.*Mona* bound for Ramsey, both engines about to make a joint,spectacular departure, racing each other to the delight of the passengers aboard their trains, until the two parallel single lines diverge en-route to their diverse destinations. The trains seem to be well patronised, but in the twelve months since your author visited the line the once neatly raked gravelled platforms have become unkempt and somewhat overgrown and there is abroad the miasma of neglect.   *G.Biddle.*

St.John's.(Peel end).c.1968. A photographer is engaged, by the level crossing, capturing the I.O.M.Rly resurgent, in the early days of Lord Ailsa's regime. A Ramsey train makes a lively exit, the plume of steam from the whistle valve signifying that, in accordance with *Rule No.245* the driver has acknowledged the guard's signal confirming his presence aboard the train. The condition of the track received attention before the railway's re-opening -it has been nicely "fettled" and reballasted, although some sleepers need renewing. The platforms look festive with pennants flying high. The area around St.John's, from ancient times has been an important crossing point where the tracks going from the east to west coast bisected those coming from the southerly Castletown direction and continued, by way of the valley of the River Neb to skirt the western edge of the Snaefell range and gain access to the shore-line near Kirkmichael and so to the north of the island.

C.L.Caddy

St.John's.c.1968. From the inception of their negotiations to lease the undertaking, the Marquess of Ailsa's group was on good terms with the Isle of Man Steam Railway Supporters Association, and it was agreed that some of their members should carry out the cosmetic restoration of engines not in use. A batch of engines was stored in the carriage shed at St.John's and placed on display in the mornings, and stabled at night by the locomotive of the first and last trains of the day to work through. The line-up features the former Manx Northern's *Caledonia*, carrying her I.O.M.Rly No.**15** on the chimney and the inscription *M.N.R. CALEDONIA.No.4* on the side-tanks. Also present were No.**16**. *Mannin*. No.**6**. *Peveril*. No.**1**. *Sutherland* and No.**14**. *Thornhill*, formerly as their No.**3**. the Manx Northern's only Beyer Peacock engine: *Thornhill* is still resident on the island, in private ownership.

C.L.Caddy

St.John's. 21st September. 1962. In the distance the Down Home signal is seen to be lowered and the ex County Donegal railcars are negotiating the level crossing in a working from Peel, as Mrs Crellin, wife of Stationmaster George Crellin operates the 'Stevens Patent' signal levers. For some years a footbridge spanned the tracks at this end of the station, but it was demolished during the drive for 'scrap-iron' in the early days of World War II. When the Winter Timetables were published, at short notice, to take effect from Monday, 24th September 1962, it specified that there was to be only one, daily return trip (at mid-day) between Douglas and Port Erin and this would be steam hauled. A similar service would be worked between Douglas and Peel using the railcars, coupled back-to-back and they could, in addition, haul goods vehicles as necessary.   *Norman Jones.*

Nr. St.John's. Saturday 21st September. 1963. We stayed at The Abbey, Mrs E.Quayle's very comfortable and homely guest house (seen in rear) situated ¾ miles from Peel and Herbert and I carried out an unofficial track inspection. The sleepers were past their 'sell-by' date, although the rails were not bad, with few signs of corrosion or side-cutting. They told us at St.John's that spoil from the Foxdale mines was used to 'top-up' the original ballast - it had certainly compacted into a most solid formation. A civil engineering survey of 1965 reported that the rails, of various weights e.g. 56 lbs, 60 lbs, and 65 lbs, were good for some years but concern was expressed about the state of the sleepers. In 1967 the first consignment of 5,000 new sleepers arrived. I was interested to discover that Rule No.295 of the I.O.M.Rly's Rule Book referred to Platelayers trolleys as "lorries" - A phrase I had not encountered in general use previously excepting by my Uncle Bob Jones, a retired Chief Inspector and Herbert Woodward, who were old Cheshire Lines men.

Photo: The late Herbert Woodward.

Peel.12th August.1963. For a mid-summer afternoon the station is deserted, except for a youthful photographer with his attention centered on No.**5**.*Mona*. The is here almost a panoramic view of the precincts, including the commodious and purpose built Goods Shed and Platform, and, standing by the bay platform interesting brake/compo.carriage,at the Douglas end of the stabled rake. It is an example of the F40-44 series purchased during 1908/9 to handle the extra traff accruing from the I.O.M.Rly's absorption of the Manx Northern Railway, whose mainly six-wheeled coaches were built to James Cleminson's system, with speci sets of axles and truck gear. The central pair of wheels had lateral play;the front and rear axles were pivoted and connected to the central axle and wheels by radi links. Built by the Swansea Wagon Co.Ltd. in 1879 they were well out-dated by 1904 when the senior company took over.   *G.Biddl*

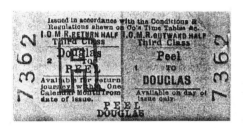

Peel. This post-war, atmospheric scene features 2-4-0T.No.**6**.*Peveril* (Works No.1524 of 1875) with glistening dome and an overall condition indicative of 'tender loving care' both in the shops and by her crew. The well-chosen lowish camera angle invests Peveril with a forceful air but, even so, she is somewhat overpowered by the colossus of a water tank, which is raised on an equally prodigous stone base. The gates are seen to be closed over the Mill Road level crossing, whilst the usual concourse of itinerant gulls wait on the apex of the fish curing factory for any hand-outs that are on offer.
Lens of Sutton.

Peel.c.1967.No.15 *Caledonia* is in action shunting the yard, the level crossing gates are closed to road traffic, although a wicket is free for pedestrians to use. The area around the station was traditionally associated with fish processing and the smoking and curing houses, where the famous Manx Kipper was (and still is) produced, however, during the 1960's new buildings were erected for the treatment and deep-freezing of escallops and prawns, whilst deep-freeze meat storage plants were also established. The causeway viewed across the neck of the harbour led to Peel Castle, where may be found Fenella's Tower, associated with the works of the novelist Sir Walter Scott.

C.L.Caddy.

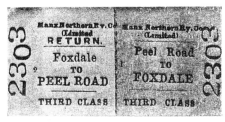

Peel.July.1962.It is always of interest to see well known buildings from an unusual angle, as is the case with this aspect of the rear elevations of the Locomotive Shed and Water Tower, which were tucked in a corner of the yard near the East Quay and Mill Road level crossing; the gasometer is another 'period.' feature. The enclosure has obviously been quite extensively cultivated as an allotment at some period, although overgrown when the photograph was taken.

D.Ibbotson.

Peel. July 1962. The hands of the station clock point to 2.20 pm and the I.O.M.Rly's No.**8.** *Fenella* has arrived with a train from Douglas via St. John's. The leading vehicle is F20, one of the two Composites with three separate Third Class compartments plus a luggage and properly enclosed Guard's portion. The projecting housing which enclosed the brake operating wheel in the van is just visible despite the escaping steam; end windows were not fitted to this class of carriage, the Guard getting a forward view through through the projecting ducket. The wall of the goods shed is embellished by several colourful and quite vintage signs, especially the two advertising *SWAN VESTAS*, and *PETTER OIL ENGINES*.   *D.Ibbotson.*

Peel. May. 1962. Coach F4 stands on the siding at Peel, opposite to the Goods Platform and Cattle Dock, which show an economical use of redundant materials in the form of the platform's protective edging, being composed of 'pensioned off' lengths of old rail. F34 was one of the batch of six 35ft long x 7ft wide bogie carriages from Messrs Brown Marshalls, following on from the early four wheelers, the bogie coaches which had Guards' compartments were fitted with brakes which acted on all eight of the wheels.
          D.Ibbotson.

Peel. 20th September. 1962. Accompanying the River Neb on it's journey to the sea the railway entered the environs of Peel, passing in addition to the curing houses, the remains of the old rope-walk, the power station and a brick works. Having carefully negotiated the Mill Road level crossing, Driver Jimmy Kneale of Ramsey takes the ex C.D. Railcars gently towards the buffer-stops, whilst Jack Watterson of Port Erin looks out from the vehicle's rear. At the leading end the white central body stripe dips in a chevron whereas at the Douglas end the line is unbroken. The Goods Shed, Goods Platform and Cattle Dock lay to the left of the slab edged, gravel surfaced platform; a former Manx Northern Railway van is stabled on the siding close to the Cattle Dock. *Norman Jones.*

Peel. 20th September 1962. Ex County Donegal Railcar - Driver Jack Watterson appreciated the refinements of a windscreen wiper, sliding windows, a comfortable seat and good driving position. To the right lies Corrin's Hill (485ft) famous for its Tower, or Folly, built by Mr Corrin a wealthy Nonconformist whose wife and family pre-deceased him and were buried on unconsecrated ground near his Tower. On his death he was buried in the churchyard, against his wishes, but had arranged with four friends if this happened to dig his body up and bury it near those of his family. This, they did, but before they got to the top of the hill it was dawn so they hid the coffin under a hedge, and returned the next night to finish the job.
Norman Jones.

Peel. 20th September 1962. The station lay in a triangular area, the sides represented by the East Quay and Mill Road and the base the shorter Lake Road, named after the saltings from which the station site was reclaimed. Having unloaded their passengers the railcars visited the goods yard to collect the partly loaded Wagon No.M56 and returned with it to the passenger platform to complete its loading with general goods from the parcels office. During World War I a British Government Prisoner of War/Detention Camp was set up at Knockaloe on the southern side of Corrin's Hill near to the village of Patrick, and a branch 1 mile 6 chains long was laid down to end at the quayside at Peel, so that detainees could walk straight from the boats to the trains. The branch was worked by the I.O.M.Rly under a Government agreement, No.15 Caledonia proving her worth as the most powerful locomotive available, was based at Peel to work the Knockaloe Branch which was steeply graded and posessed many sharp curves and was not easy to operate. The branch was lifted in the early 1920's.					*Norman Jones.*

Peel. 20th September.1962. Beyond the station can be descried St.Patrick's Isle, with the Round Tower and Castle to left of centre, nearer at hand the handy Harbour Snack bar, a favourite haunt for photographers in the 60's. Seed Potatoes, visitor's cabin trunks and gas cylinders are amongst the 'sundries' being loaded onto Wagon M56. In the immediate foreground is the ramp leading to the raised length of the platform. Against the harbour wall a highway lighting standard sprouts a tramway style side-arm bracket, whilst the perimeter railings of the station display a bold pattern of ball and spike finials. The drain from roof and awnings is piped down the centre of the awning support column, to discharge into the drain by means of a spout at the base of the plinth, all very ornate with some quite exquisite tracery and indicative of the skill of workers in iron at that time. Architectural flamboyance of this type is the hallmark of wealthy and expanding societies - this was the period when 'Made in Britain' was accepted, world-wide as a manifestation of supreme quality in materials, workmanship and design.					*Norman Jones.*

Glen Mooar. 21st September.1963. The sediments of Ordovician origin which form three quarters of the mass of the Isle of Man were laid down about 400 million years ago, during the Caledonian Mountain Building period. The masses of North Barrule (1860ft), Snaefell (2034ft), Bein-y-Phot,and lesser prominences are formed mainly of Manx Slate. To circumvent the mountains the railway surveyors chose a route for the Manx Northern line by way of the western coast, even so some significant works were entailed. The viaduct at Glen Mooar was built following World War I by Messrs. Francis Morton & Co.Ltd., to replace the original life-expired structure. From the south the line fell at 1 in 100 to the lattice steel viaduct, about 75ft above river level. The three 60ft spans were supported on 60ft high piers. Nearby was a small plate-layers hut, one of a number erected on the M.N.Rly to a design which would have permitted their conversion to a rural station if need arose. The rails have been lifted, the girders have been removed and little but the remains of the piers are still extant.

Photo:The Late Herbert Woodward.

Kirkmichael. Wednesday. 28th August.1968. No.10.*G.H.Wood* takes on water. Beside the supply column is John Wright, whilst Frank Shepherd, ex Heaton Mersey Shed peers through the cab window. Kirkmichael Station Master, Mr Fred Caley is in charge. Mr Caley joined the I.O.M.Rly when local farmers still travelled by pony and trap to the station; one of Fred's first jobs was to watch the horses and vehicles whilst their masters were away. Kirkmichael, the largest village in the north-west is well known as a T.T.vantage point but the local people are trapped when the roads are closed on race days. There was an escape route when the Ramsey-St.John's railway line was open. In 1991 the Michael Commissioners initiated a feasibility study to examine the requirements for building a new exit road. The cost might be between £250,000 to £500,000 and would use the abandoned route of the M.N.Rly between Glen Wyllin and Rhencullan.The latter is also known in T.T. circles as 'Birkin's Bend.' In 1927 roads were not closed during practice and Archie Birkin (brother of 'Tim'a famous racing car driver) was killed in a collision with a motor van, leading to Tynwald introducing legislation to enforce compulsory closure of the roads to general traffic when racing was taking place.

P.H.Abell.

Ballaugh.c.1950. Driver Percy Cain is oiling round former Manx Northern Rly.2-4-0T *Thornhill*, named after the home of the M.N.R's Chairman John Thomas Clucas Esq. The locomotive was built as Beyer Peacock's Works No.2028 of 1880, her two predecessors the Sharp Stewart engines did not receive their names of Ramsey and Northern until 1893. No.**14** is working forward to Ramsey the level crossing at Ballaugh (pronounced 'Billarf' or Berlarf')just out of sight to the right.The station had a long Passing Loop and through Goods Siding a Cattle Dock, Goods Platform and Goods Shed.The Up Home signal was 'slotted'; a Stevens signal lever was located near to the station building with a standard type on the approach side of the level crossing. The Down Home signal arm,originally a fish-tail semaphore was cut short about 1950.

John Radcliffe, English Life Publications:
P.H.Abell collection.

Ballacrye.Wednesday.18th July.1962. Trains proceeding towards Ramsey after leaving Ballaugh next encountered this level crossing, where we me No.**10**.*G.H.Wood*, running bunker-first, hurrying a two coach train in the direction of St.John's over a rather overgrown section of track. The driver has just sounde the obligatory 'prolonged whistle blast', to which the lady crossing keeper responds by exhibiting a white 'all clear' signal flag.The bystanders are the Tourist Board' Mr Jack Cretney and the late Herbert Woodward. When the Marquess of Ailsa took charge on 1st April 1967 it was not long before a revised Rule Book was produce which specified 'green' instead of 'white' as the 'all clear' signal. The line's new General Manager was reported to have made the comment 'too many childre wave white handkerchiefs'.   *Norman Jones*

Ballacrye.18th July.1962. No.**10**.*G.H.Wood* rattled over the crossing in fine style and we returned to the Tourist Board's van (observed parked in the lane) fo a visit to nearby Glen Helen,a delightful place once part of the Rhenass Estate. It later passed to a Mr Marsden, of Liverpool who named it after his daughter. I is a typical Manx glen, with a tumbling water-fall near the waters' meet of two lovely streams, the Rhenass and Blabar.In the 1870's the Glen was served by a (long closed)halt sited near to Ballacraine level crossing,the trains were met by horse-drawn conveyances from the pleasure grounds.   *Norman Jones*

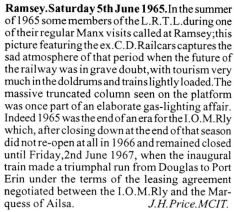

Ramsey. Saturday 5th June 1965. In the summer of 1965 some members of the L.R.T.L. during one of their regular Manx visits called at Ramsey; this picture featuring the ex.C.D.Railcars captures the sad atmosphere of that period when the future of the railway was in grave doubt, with tourism very much in the doldrums and trains lightly loaded. The massive truncated column seen on the platform was once part of an elaborate gas-lighting affair. Indeed 1965 was the end of an era for the I.O.M.Rly which, after closing down at the end of that season did not re-open at all in 1966 and remained closed until Friday, 2nd June 1967, when the inaugural train made a triumphal run from Douglas to Port Erin under the terms of the leasing agreement negotiated between the I.O.M.Rly and the Marquess of Ailsa.   *J.H.Price.MCIT.*

Ramsey. 12th August 1963. Ramsey was considered (certainly by its inhabitants) to be the second most important town on the island so, as the promoters of the M.N.Rly were, barring one, local men one would expect it to be the headquarters of the new railway. Not so! Although provision was made for offices within the station buildings alternative premises were found in Douglas, from where operations were conducted. The Manx Government took up some shares and the Board of Trade's Inspecting Officer of Railways, Col.F.H.Rich was appointed as Governing Director. We recall that visits by members of the Inspectorate to Manx Railways and Tramways were by invitation only; there was no statutory obligation. The 'Northern' line never made much money and by 1963 the general air of malaise is evident. Even so Ramsey immortalised the 'country station' as exemplified by the tin-plate creations of Messrs.Hornby and their contemporaries. The Workshops, Loco Shed, Goods Shed and Water Tank were all to the right of the picture, as was the station yard, which contained a cart weighbridge.
                  G.Biddle.

Ramsey. Monday 12th August 1963. A panoramic view, this, of the former Manx Northern Rly terminal; of particular modelling interest is a definitive view of the only signal on the site. It was similar to those installed at other of the Manx Northern's stations, although not St.John's. To guard against working errors, or improper use, two slot detectors were fitted between the points; a Stevens Signal Lever was located on the platform. The signal lamp is intact, although lacking a spectacle lens and the splendid finial is much to be admired. The water-tower and large corrugated-iron carriage shed occupy the left-hand side of the picture. The station buildings (centre) were built by a local firm Messrs Boyde Brothers, the stations, the lay-out and even rolling stock were designed by W.H.Thomas Esq.,M.I.C.E.,M.I.M.E.of London,who supervised the construction, although a Mr Malcolm Grant-Dalton was the resident engineer.
G.Biddle.

Ramsey.Wednesday 19th April 1950. Former Manx Northern Rly.engine No.**3**.*Thornhill*,renumbered as I.O.M.Rly No.**14**,in fine condition, poses beside the former M.N.Rly's Locomotive Shed and Workshop buildings;shortly after they took over the 'Northern' line the I.O.M.Rly centralised all the facilities for major engine overhauls at their Douglas shops. The first two M.N.Rly engines were from Messrs Sharp Stewart, but Messrs Beyer Peacock produced No.3. as their Works No.2028 in 1880. In 1921 the small 2ft 10.3/4ins diameter boiler, pressed to 120 lbs was replaced by one of 3ft 3ins diameter, working at 160 lbs pressure;this was the last boiler to be fitted with Salter safety valves supplied to the Isle of Man Railway, about 1960 the stately Beyer Peacock chimney was replaced by a shorter, cast-iron one.
The late H.C.Casserley:courtesy Richard Casserley.